S0-ACN-102

CURE OF MIND
and
CURE OF SOUL

By the same author

HOLINESS IS WHOLENESS
and Other Essays
INDIVIDUATION

CURE OF MIND
and
CURE OF SOUL

Depth Psychology and
Pastoral Care

ASSOCIATED MENNONITE BIBLICAL SEMINARIES GOSHEN LIBRARY

by

JOSEF GOLDBRUNNER

THE UNIVERSITY OF NOTRE DAME PRESS • 1962

GOSHEN COLLEGE LIBRARY
GOSHEN, INDIANA

This translation from the original German, Personale
Seelsorge, *2nd edition,* 1955 (*Verlag Herder,
Freiburg, Germany*) *was made by*
STANLEY GODMAN

NIHIL OBSTAT: JOANNES M. T. BARTON, S.T.D., L.S.S.
CENSOR DEPVTATVS
IMPRIMATVR: ✠ GEORGIVS L. CRAVEN
EPISCOPVS SEBASTOPOLIS
VICARIVS GENERALIS
WESTMONASTERII: DIE XII MAII MCMLVIII

201.6
G57e
BR
110
G 6.13

© 1962 UNIVERSITY OF NOTRE DAME PRESS
NOTRE DAME, IND.

First published in England by Burns, Oates and Washbourne Ltd. 1958
First Paperback Printing July   1962
Second Paperback Printing May   1963
Third Paperback Printing September 1964

03265

PREFACE

THE present work has arisen from the encounter between depth psychology and the cure of souls which has now been taking place, in theory and practice, for many years.

The great obstacle to the realization of faith in the present age is the levelling influence of the masses. All the more need, then, for those concerned with the cure of souls to turn their attention to the opposite pole which resides in the innermost heart of man, that is, the person.

By taking the concept of the person as a criterion it is possible to incorporate the positions of depth psychology in the Christian conception of man, but in the process the weaknesses in the psychological position are also exposed. Once it is freed, however, from its one-sided emphasis on the diseased soul, it can provide us with a new vision of the personal life and be fruitfully applied at all stages of religious education.

The reader is assumed to be aware of the basic phenomena of depth psychology as expounded, for example, in my book *Individuation*. The ideas discussed in that work are developed here but without reference to a specific author and with different presuppositions in mind.

The first part is devoted mainly to theory, the

5

second to practice, though a few overlappings proved to be unavoidable.

I should like to acknowledge my indebtedness to the work of Dr Theodor Müncker, Professor of Moral Theology at the University of Freiburg and of Professor Josef Sellmair, Professor of Religious Education at the University of Munich.

CONTENTS

PART ONE

PART TWO

7

PART ONE

1. HUMANITY AND CHRISTIANITY

It is becoming ever clearer that the most important problem facing the Catholic priest to-day is the problem of faith. In conversations about the Faith the primary concern is not the justification or defence of the Faith, nor is the main emphasis on intellectual understanding. It is faith as a way and form of life that is sought after, dimly descried or evaded to-day. The attitude of the unbeliever, the seeker and also of the conscious believer aspiring to greater heights of faith, is therefore different from what it was in the previous century. It is fuller, more comprehensive, more completely human. The difference may be seen in three ways.

There is in the first place the condition of those who are simply unable to believe because they have a complete lack of feeling for "religious" things. Their religious sense is undeveloped, impeded, unco-operative or degenerate. They regard religious ideas as mere theories utterly out of touch with real life. In the second place there is the situation of the genuine seeker after religion whose questionings arise not from rational scepticism but from a deeper concern: he is worried about the changes Christianity may bring about in him if he accepts it, changes not only in the intellectual sphere but in the realms of feeling and acting, of social relationships and personal behaviour. Finally, there is the alert believer who is impelled by a yearning for a life rooted in the fullness of religion, longing to deepen his experience of the substance of the Faith, because he has already had a taste of the Truth in the truest sense of the word.

Faith has a deeper influence than knowledge, it effects more far-reaching changes than a purely external reorientation based on a reassessment of ethical values. Faith exerts its influence on man above all at the very centre of the person from which all his abilities and dispositions are directed. Christianity is confronted by the whole of the human personality. In the encounter between man and the Faith there is a mutual challenge.

The subject of this book is the particular situation and nature of this relationship at the present time. The investigation of the psychic preconditions of the super-natural virtue of faith, of the qualities that make it possible for the conscience to make a decision for Christianity and for a life of faith to grow out of that decision—such an investigation has its part, albeit one of secondary importance, in the *analysis fidei*.

The problem of the way in which man's human nature can be opened up and developed to meet the Gospel and the way its "material" can be brought in touch with the supernatural is one of the concerns of religious education. We do not mean, what is now taken for granted in educational theory, that education must take into account the child's or adult's particular stage of development and powers of understanding, and that the teaching material must be prepared accordingly. In contrast to the kind of religious education which uses the results of secular theory and merely "applies" them to religious teaching whilst still moving on the same level as secular education, our purpose here is to consider both the values to be taught (i.e. the Faith) and the learner from a specifically Christian point of view.

The Christian faith does not belong to the same category as culture, ethics, aesthetics and natural religiosity.[1] There are connections between all of these but the life of Christian faith is based on values of a quite different quality. Similarly, the "level of being" is different when faith is exerting its influence on man to when man is responding to a work of art. The categories are the natural and the supernatural, with all their differences and inter-relationships. The supernatural is a personal Being, which implies that faith is a relationship between man and the God who appeared in Christ and is now invisible. Faith is a call and a summons from God and the process by which man answers the call. What occurs in this process and how this faith operates has a much deeper influence on man than is demonstrated by the psychology of evolution and the usual educational theories. Faith as a

[1] By natural religiosity we mean the worship of the numinous which is found in some form or other in all peoples. Natural religion proceeds upwards from below, whereas primitive revealed religion proceeds from above downwards. Cf. Chapter 9 of the present work.

personal process appeals to man as a person. Catholic education ought to serve this process and direct its endeavours towards the development of man as person.

If the personal view of the Faith is given a central place, a corresponding conception of man as person will be required. Humanity and Christianity, anthropology and theology, man and faith all converge when viewed from the aspect of the personal.

2. THE PERSONAL

IN his intercourse with men and women to-day the priest realizes that the influence of his work is decreasing because the legacy of a Christian atmosphere from the centuries of faith is gradually dwindling away. The people in the pews are no longer a body of Christian "people" but mere individuals, a multiplicity of individuals who wish to be addressed as individuals. As a result effective pastoral work is shifting more and more to the purely personal level. Even though the personal note was never absent, to-day there is a special emphasis on this demand for and turning towards the personal. The process of "massification" in civil and political life is levelling down the personal element and evoking a counter-movement devoted to the cultivation of the unique life of the individual person. The personal sphere is becoming the subject of theoretical and practical investigation in a new and deeper way.

1.   Created Being is constituted in two fundamental modes: the mode of nature and the mode
of the personal. All a-personal life is natural, including human life which consists of a nature
based on body and soul. This is important since,
although man is metaphysically a person, he can
also live a-personally or pre-personally, i.e. on the
purely natural plane, insofar as he merely acts
instinctively and not responsibly. It is man's task
to permeate his whole nature with the personal, by
bringing all his predispositions and abilities under
its rule. It is the purpose of the present work to
indicate ways and means of achieving this.

2.   The Person is individual spiritual being,[1] so
that one may also say that the person is the individual in the spiritual order. Every person is unique
and irreplaceable. This is the foundation of his
incomparable dignity and status in society, which
prohibits him being used as a mere means to an
end. The life of the community ought be be so
ordered that it is possible for personal life to develop in it.[2]

3.   The person is the "possessor"[3] of all the
expressions of man's life, the vehicle of his nature.
It thinks with his mind, sees through his eyes,
touches with his hands: thus it holds the whole of

[1] Boethius's definition runs: *"persona est rationalis
naturae individua substantia"* (*De Duabus nat.*, c. I).
[2] Cf. Chapters 7 and 8 of the present work.
[3] In scholastic terminology the "substance" and
"subsistence" of the person.

human nature together, it is its unifying principle and centre. Nature, on the other hand, serves to express the life of the person, it is the "material" by which the person expresses itself in the world.

According to a Christian philosophy of life religious education must therefore not only take into account the fact that the person must rule over nature and be its centre, it must also study the predispositions of the body and especially of the soul in order to be able to suggest how the person can express itself through them. If the person is to use human nature and "play on it as on an instrument" it is necessary to know the laws of the physical and especially the spiritual constitution and to submit to them as the pianist submits to the keyboard of the piano. The present work examines how the new findings of depth psychology on the life of the soul can be used in the formation of the person so that the person may express itself completely within its own nature.

4. The person is the beginning and end of all the expressions of life; all thinking, speaking and doing should take the person as its point of departure and all listening and receiving should seek it as its true goal. But the person itself is the mysterious centre which reposes, in an odd way, in itself, incomprehensibly, albeit bearing responsibility. Although the character of a man often suggests how he will act in a given situation, no one knows for certain what his final decision will be: the person is a mysterious and genuinely

creative beginning, i.e. it belongs to itself and is free. When we speak figuratively of the "core of the person" we mean the centre which is the bearer of responsibility, which has the free capacity for decision and is the essence of the human being. Insofar as a human being succeeds in acting from the centre of his person, he rises above the natural determination of his nature and can no longer be explained in terms of psychology and biology; he lives in the realm of personal freedom.[1]

5. The dimensions of upper and lower hold good in the a-personal realm of Being. The upper is the light, the sky; the lower is the dark, the earth, the heavy. There is an upper and lower in human nature too. The upper is the intellect, the lower is the instincts. Value judgements are often bound up with this sense of the upper and lower.

The spiritual and personal sphere, however, is orientated inwards: the alternative is either to live from within or to be determined from without. The more personally a man lives, the more he is bound up with his inner life. The "core of the person" is as it were the interior of the self.

6. The person is a self-contained whole, but it is not shut off from other persons. It is made for relationships with the Thou. Part of its very nature is to "be with the Thou". The ego is awakened to life in relationship with the Thou, for the relation between persons is different from the relation

[1] Cf. the present work, p. 102.

between a person and a non-ego, it is not merely a confrontation of subject and object.[1] When the space between two persons is filled with trust, love, affection or even with the opposite of these, a personal contact takes place, a spiritual contact which is more inward than a relation between things, or between a person and a thing or an animal. Religious education therefore needs an atmosphere in which personal relationships can thrive.[2]

7.   In connection with the concept of the person that of the personality thrusts itself on our attention. Both concepts must be distinguished but their connection must also be borne in mind. Personality is first of all the external appearance of a human being, it is the "form of the living individuality".[3] According to Steinbüchel, "Person is an ontological content of being, personality an axiological content of value".[4] According to him the genuine personality is shaped and bounded in four directions: "as the life of spiritual individuality; as the intention of a firm character; as the penetration of the total approach to life by the integral personality; and as the readiness for sacrificial service to the Being in which it stands". The personality is finally defined "as the person which

[1] Unless a person merely "observes" another, merely takes him as an object of knowledge and enters into no personal relationship with him.
[2] Chapters 8 and 12 of the present work.
[3] Romano Guardini, *Welt und Person*, Würzburg, 1939, p. 128.
[4] Theodor Steinbüchel, *Die philosophische Grundlegung der katholischen Sittenlehre*, vol. II, Düsseldorf, 1938.

effects and sustains the good". Personality is the fulfilment of personal being.

Now it is possible for someone to appear to be a personality, with a marked and well-known character of his own, and yet still remain entirely or partly in the pre-personal sphere, being determined, for example, by strong instinctive dispositions or by the fashionable tendencies of the time so that he is actually no more than a pseudo-personality.[1] This has led to a mistrustful attitude to the iridescent concept of personality which has been heightened still further by the historical taint attached to the concept. In religious education, therefore, it would be better to think in terms of a doctrine of the life of the person rather than the "culture of the personality".

8. Existentialism has emphasized a particular feature in the structure of the person.[2] Although he is endowed with the preconditions requisite for

---

[1] The various factors which go to the formation of a pseudo-personality will be discussed in Chapter 5 of the present work.

[2] The point of departure in the main representatives of existential philosophy varies. In his "theology of existence" Kierkegaard is concerned with the self-understanding of the Christian; Karl Jaspers circles around the existence of man; in Heidegger the interpretation of human existence is wholly subservient to the problem of Being. Despite their variety, however, they all have an anthropological reference in their emphasis on the dynamic factor in the structure of the person and that is the only thing that interests us in the present context. *Literature*: Kierkegaard: *Sickness unto Death*, Evans-Lowrie, London, 1941; Heidegger, *Sein und Zeit*, 1927, and *Holzwege*, 1950; Jaspers, *Philosophie*, 1932.

the formation of a person man can also live a-
personally. How is this possible and what is the
particular aspect of the human structure to which
it is due?

The person is able and is under a necessity to
form an opinion about itself. Mass existence, however, tends to drown man in the flood of daily life,
causing him merely to drift along and not live in
and out of himself at all. The result is that he never
takes root in himself, he does not live from himself
at all but is absorbed in the anonymous consciousness of the mass; he does not make decisions for
himself, his decisions are made for him by the
mind of the mass.[1] He himself, i.e. his own person,
cannot express itself. This sort of man does not
fully exist at all.

A person does not exist like a piece of wood, a
tree or a house which is determined by place, size
and age.[2] In order that a person may really speak
out of itself, be present and "exist", it must do
something with itself: it must acquire itself, take
hold of itself, actuate itself. Only then does man
"exist" in the full sense of the word. This "existence", which is the opposite of merely being
present, is man's sole prerogative as a personal
being. It implies a taking hold of oneself and de-
ciding for oneself what one's life is to be (Kierke-

[1] Heidegger describes this condition as *"Verfallen"*,
"unauthenticity", "forgetfulness of Being", "merely
being present". The understanding of Being is "concealed" and "deadened".

[2] *Dasein* as opposed to *Sosein*, according to the scholastic theory.

gaard). Existence means the realization of one's being as a self (Jaspers), projecting oneself into real being (*ex-sistere*) and having understanding of Being (Heidegger). In his capacity for free decision man rises above the mere state of nature and becomes the person which he is from birth. The existential and the personal permeate each other.[1]

9. As a personal being man is confronted with a task. It is his task to realize his existence. To do this it is necessary that he should wake up to his real nature, be wrenched out of the security and solidity of his everyday routine and attain to his own reality.

This process develops into the "taking hold" of existence, which is also called self-realization. As it takes place something happens in the person. It forms ideas about itself; it is roused to life as a person and begins to penetrate the whole being of man. The essential being of the person finds expression and is transformed into actuality.[2] The person is "actuated". In this context human

[1] In Kierkegaard the stages on this way are the progress from the aesthetic, through the ethical, to the religious stage; in Jaspers the frontier situations, especially death, suffering, struggle and guilt; in Heidegger fear drives man to existence through the transitory phases. We are only concerned here with the problem of the realization of the person so that the differences we have mentioned will not be taken into account.

[2] To obviate the danger of a dissolution of the person in mere actuality, as sometimes seems possible in existential philosophy, it should be pointed out that in our context the actual is seen as the development of the condition of being. Within the metaphysical and static

development signifies the attainment of a personal attitude through the activation of personal being and this attitude stamps and sustains man's whole nature.

10. However we describe this process: the actuating of the person, the process of becoming authentic, the taking hold of existence, self-realization, self-development—it inevitably forces us to re-think the problem of character training. It sets the person at the centre of educational activity and makes personal relationships the criterion of a fruitful approach to educational problems.[1]

11. What has just been said applies even more to religious education which is charged with the duty of helping the "children of God" to ripen into "sons" and "daughters" of God. Just as the concept "child of God" occupies a key position in pastoral theology by reason of the emphasis laid on the reality of baptism ("reborn", "begotten" of God the Father and Mother Church), the concepts

concept of the person such as we find in scholastic thought this development reveals a dynamic side in the structure of the person.

[1] Though there is a danger of the term being treated as a slogan it may be said that the modern "education for wholeness" must be deepened into "personal education", the person being the principle which sums up in itself the wholeness of spiritual life. "Personal education" does not, however, aim merely at the summing up of the human but strives to advance from a purely humanistic conception of the development of human predispositions to life which is based on a wholly personal attitude.

"sons"[1] and "daughters" of God must also be taken seriously. What we have in mind is the personal relationship of a grown-up son to his father, to whom he is tied by the bonds of respect and friendship, whom he serves and to whom he is responsible. The reality, difficulty, sobriety and fulfilment of a relationship between the Father-God and the human being raised to the status of son or daughter[2] should be regarded in the light of the natural, cultivated relationship between a father and his grown-up children.

12.   In terms of religious education this means that every natural personal relationship should be regarded as an opportunity for the actuating of the person, for the training of a personal character and as the pre-condition and first step towards the reality of the maturing relationship to the invisible God, who discloses his paternal status in revelation. Personal existence and the word of revelation, humanity and Christianity enter into a relationship of mutual tension and man's personal relationship to God should grow increasingly from their combination. The intensification of this relationship is the sign of a living faith, of a faith which commands not merely the intellect and the will but the whole man. This process, which can be called the "realization" of faith,[3] is the subject of the present work.

[1] Cf. Matt. 5, 9.   [2] Luke 15, 20 and 22-24.
[3] The concept of "Realization" coincides with the term "realize" as used by Newman. This is a central concept in his theory of faith. It may be interpreted as

13.   In its search for help in the solution of this problem religious education comes upon depth psychology, since this too is, like existential philosophy, concerned with the self-understanding of man, from the point of view not of knowledge, but of experience. Depth psychology attempts to show how existence can be taken hold of, how the person is actuated, how man can become authentic. Depth psychology translates the findings of existential philosophy into terms of immediate experience. Insofar, therefore, as depth psychology serves the development of a personalistic view of man, it is important for the realization of the life of faith, since it embraces man in his "depths" and makes it possible to summon the whole nature of man and bring it into relation with Christianity.

3.   DEPTH PSYCHOLOGY

As a figurative term the concept of depth psychology is one-sided. It embraces the psychological

---

the great "transformer" where an idea or a thought is converted into a spiritual reality in man. Purely intellectual knowledge is so worked up that it can really live and create within us. Inner realization pushes on into external action and thus knowledge ultimately achieves personal realization. There is as yet no monograph on Newman's theory of "realizing". The best account of it in Newman's own work will be found in *An Essay in Aid of a Grammar of Assent*. Whereas Newman deals with the philosophical and theological aspects of the "realization of faith", in the present context we are interested in the psychological preconditions of realization.

findings of psychotherapy,[1] from which it developed. It is now possible, however, to say that depth psychology has various fields of application. Psychotherapy is the most advanced and differentiated of these; but in various countries it has already gained a footing in education.[2]

In pastoral work the use of depth psychology appeared to begin in connection with confession, above all with reference to the freeing of those haunted by scruples from the confessional. But in order to demonstrate the full range of the profit which can be derived from depth psychology

[1] Psychotherapy was established by Freud round the turn of the century as an independent science alongside and often even against psychiatry. The aim of psychotherapy is to heal, even to heal physical disease by treating the soul. Its basic axiom, which has been proved many times by experience, is that spiritual factors are capable of making man physically ill. The spiritual causes usually lie in the unconscious; to discover them needs a clear-cut method. The great development of psychotherapy proceeded from Freud (his theory is called psychoanaylsis) through Adler (individual psychology) to Jung (analytical psychology). The connection with existential philosophy was established by Viktor Frankl (logotherapy) and Ludwig Binswanger (analysis of existence). There are already signs of a "personalistic analysis" in the work of Igor Caruso. *Literature:* Sigmund Freud, *Introductory Lectures on Psychoanalysis, Collected Works,* Vol. 16, London, 1950; Alfred Adler, *Menschenkenntnis,* Leipzig, 1928; C. G. Jung, *Two Essays in Analytical Psychology, Collected Works,* Vol. 7, London, 1954; Viktor Frankl, *Psychoanalyse und Synthese der Existenz,* Freiburg, 1952; Josef Goldbrunner, *Individuation,* Notre Dame, 1964.

[2] U.S.A. and Sweden, though only in accordance with the teaching of Freud and Adler. There is great interest among practising teachers in Germany.

in the cure of souls it is necessary to show (1) its place in the history of anthropology, (2) its application to a personalistic view of man and (3) its ontological foundations.

1 (a). Right up to our own time the Cartesian view of man has had the greatest influence. It singles out one human capacity, the intellectual, and bases its whole valuation of man thereon. Man is conceived as *res cogitans*. He is separated by a gulf from the world, the *res extensa*. A straight line leads from Descartes to Kant, Fichte and Hegel. A completely one-sided rationalistic view of man as consisting wholly of theoretical understanding and reasonable will was adopted.

(b) Darwin's discovery of the evolutionary laws of organisms directed attention to the connection between man and the animal world and led to an attempt to explain man "from below" (Darwin, Haeckel). Anthropology was reduced to a branch of zoology. Man was defined as a "defective being"—in comparison with the animals.[1]

(c) Despite the one-sidedness of these zoological theories it must be recognized that they extended our knowledge of human nature though they merely laid bare one stratum in the structure of man.[2] A further extension was brought about, in reaction to the Cartesian view of man, by the emphasis which Freud and Klages laid on the

[1] Arnold Gehlen, *Der Mensch, seine Natur und seine Stellung in der Welt*, 1950.

[2] Their one-sidedness consists in their desire to explain the whole of man from this one point of view.

24

irrational subsoil. Freud rediscovered the "earthy depths" of human nature but his sexual theory was not incorporated in an emancipating view of the whole of human nature. He degraded the unconscious to the level of a "depository" of the morally bad, a mere "wastepaper basket" of inferiorities and complexes. Ludwig Klages[1] bases his view of man on a conviction of the fundamental opposition between *Logos* and *Bios*, thought and experience, mind and soul. The mind is the "adversary" of the soul. Jung was the first to succeed in overcoming the dualism between the rational and the irrational thereby doing justice to the true reality of human nature.

To sum up, it may be said that all references to the irrational in man, whether under the guise of the "soul" as in Klages or the "unconscious" of the psychotherapists, did draw attention to the totality of human nature. But the service performed by psychotherapy is to have brought to public attention the whole activity and importance of the irrational in the unconscious of the human soul; it has thereby become the most fruitful stimulus for present-day anthropology. The psychology of consciousness has been compelled to extend its concept of the soul.

(d)   The next element to be mentioned in this systematic survey of present-day anthropology is the existentialist interpretation of man. Man cannot be understood solely from a study of the whole

[1] Ludwig Klages, *Der Geist als Widersacher der Seele*, 3 vols., 1929-32.

of human nature; his relationship to the surrounding world must also be included. He is not merely confronted by his environment, he is set inside it, and neither can be understood in isolation one from the other. Man can only be understood in relation to his active involvement in his environment. Man and the world form a polar unity. Man is part of existence, right inside it.[1] In this existential view of man the Cartesian theory of two substances, man and world, has been overcome. How fruitful this view of man and world as a polar unity can be seen when it is applied to the psychological position of Jung.[2]

(e) At the same time, philosophical anthropologists have come upon the kind of being represented by the human spirit. Man as spirit is a person. The work of Max Scheler[3] and Eduard Spranger[4] should be mentioned in this connection. August Vetter[5] has even gone so far as to posit a personal being as the independent centre of human nature, in which *Bios* and *Logos*, the irrational and the rational, are integrated.

(f) Only the theologian can put all these elements together and try to understand human nature "from God's point of view". Theodor Steinbüchel has investigated the ancestry of this

[1] Cf. Karl Jaspers, *Psychologie der Weltanschauungen*, 1919; Martin Heidegger, *Sein und Zeit*, 1949.

[2] See below, p. 32.

[3] Max Scheler, *Die Stellung des Menschen im Kosmos*, 1928.

[4] Eduard Spranger, *Lebensformen*, 1930.

[5] August Vetter, *Natur und Person*, Stuttgart, 1949.

theological view of man; Romano Guardini has studied the phenomenology of the relationship between God and the human person. Man with all his roots in nature is *capax Dei*. As a creature man proceeds from God and returns to Him.

(g) Finally, we must refer to the influence on pastoral work of the view of man prevailing in a particular period. In his studies of the history of pastoral theology, Franz Xaver Arnold has shown to what extent pastoral work can be taken in tow by the current philosophy of man.[1]

We shall now try to show the contribution that depth psychology can make to religious education and in particular to the realization of the faith.

2. The point of departure from which depth psychology proceeds is the fact[2] that the psyche is not identical with consciousness but that beyond consciousness unconscious spiritual "material" leads a life of its own. It lies below the threshold

[1] Franz Xaver Arnold, *Grundsätzliches und Geschichtliches zur Theologie der Seelsorge,* Vol. II of the *Untersuchungen zur Theologie der Seelsorge,* Freiburg, 1950.

[2] "The concept 'depth psychology' gives expression to the fact that our spiritual life is not confined to what we observe on the surface of consciousness, but that it has its backgrounds and undergrounds which reach down into the unconscious and that the unconscious is just as much a part of the reality of the spiritual life as the consciously experienced", P. Lersch, *Aufbau der Person,* p. 547. We may also recall a statement of Augustine's which expresses exactly what is meant by the unconscious: "*Scis hoc, sed scire te nescis*" (*De.Trin.,* XIV 7 n. 9): "You know this but you do not know that you know it." It is in you but you do not know that it is there.

of consciousness, in the "depths of the soul" (hence the term "depth psychology"). The unconscious confronts the conscious and raises the problem of the relationship between these two halves of the soul. Jung attacked the dualistic solutions (Freud, Klages)[1] which were adapted to the rationalism at the end of the nineteenth century. His researches showed that there are valuable positive elements in the unconscious[2] and as a result of this discovery he replaced the negative evaluation of the unconscious with a positive evaluation and transformed the relationship of opposition and conflict into one of mutual supplementing; his eyes were opened to the possibility of a synthesis between the conscious and the unconscious. His synthesis is no mere addition, no mere concession but a process called Individuation,[3] which is characterized by such forces and experiences as courage, suffering, endurance, self-control, contention and intellectual effort; a process, therefore, which arouses the innermost essence of a man. In this process of maturing, the powers of the conscious and the unconscious combine in the order of precedence which corresponds to their respective value. Consciousness is committed to the objective validity of truth, but the urges of the unconscious draw it into the process of individual realization. The synthesis is achieved in a

[1] See above, p. 25.
[2] C. G. Jung, *Two Essays in Analytical Psychology, Collected Works*, Volume 7, London, 1964.
[3] Cf. Josef Goldbrunner, *Individuation*, Notre Dame, 1964.

third factor, the "Self", and this is the specifically new contribution which Jung has made which bridges the gap between previous psychology and a personalist view of man. To describe the nature and function of this third element in the human psyche it will be necessary, at any rate to begin with, to use the language of metaphor.

The self hovers like a bird over the land of the soul which lies partly in the light (consciousness), partly in the dark (the unconscious), with a twilight passage between the two (the changing threshold of consciousness). The self is able to take in the land of the soul at a single glance. It holds a quite distinct position as the third element in the soul but it is connected with the other two in a peculiar way: it is set over them, it embraces them, it unites them and guarantees their unity, albeit "unobjectively".

The dimension of the "inner" reveals a different aspect of the self. The self is enthroned in the innermost room of the castle of the soul. Its art consists in attaching to itself and co-ordinating all the inhabitants of the other spheres of the soul, in its capacity as head of the spiritual "League of nations", so that the energies of the soul are released for the full exertion of their influence. By means of its tactical, "diplomatic", "political" organizing activity the self is able to govern, to make decisions, to have the final word in the interplay of spiritual forces. The self is the innermost seat of justice in man; it represents the whole man, he is "contained" therein, he is really "himself" therein. The self is more than a purely psychological court; it is a mysterious, unanalysable in-itselfness, capable of making creative decisions. Its structure is beyond the understanding of psychology, since it is not open to analysis. It is the point which represents what I mean when I address another as "Thou", or the point where I am entirely "I". Speaking figuratively, the self is the purest representation of the "material"[1] from which the person is made; but in fact it is no longer possible to use the term "material" in this context since it is an objective concept, whereas the very essence of the person (I-ness, Thou-ness) is evinced by the self.

The person is also the "supreme" element above everything in man and must be seen in terms of the "inner" dimension. The psychological concept of the self may therefore be placed alongside the metaphysical concept of the person. Both are an expression of the same thing on different levels and to that extent the person and the self are identical. The self is the court which constitutes the core of the person; it contains within itself the mystery, the creative beginning and the "personal attitude". Self-discovery is therefore identical with the achievement of a personal attitude, with the actuating of the person and the process of becoming authentic. Individuation is the psychological process of "self-realization" which is called "taking hold of existence" on the philosophical plane.

[1] Apex of the soul, spark of the soul (*scintilla animae*), ground of the soul.

We have used the Jung ternary (consciousness—unconscious—self) as the basis of our description of the structure of the psyche, but Jung's own interpretation is different.[1] On the other hand, the great importance of his theory, which may best be summed up in the above-mentioned ternary, lies in the fact that it implies a personalist view of man. Individuation as the synthesis of consciousness and unconsciousness in the self gives tangible expression to the process of maturation or the actuating of the person.

The application of depth psychology to religious education may be formulated as follows: the psychological steps which lead to the discovery of the self also assist the actuating of the person. And since this is a precondition of the Christian relationship to God which is called faith, it is not surprising that individuation can be regarded as a criterion for the realization of the Faith.[2] This means that the life of faith is dependent on the general level of maturity which the person has reached. Any help that is given towards the maturing of the personality will also have a fruitful influence on the development of faith. Religious education will have to turn its attention increasingly to these connections between the development of personal maturity and the development of faith.

[1] See below, p. 32. Cf. also Josef Goldbrunner, *Individuation*.

[2] Theodor Müncker once expressed the same thing in a lecture: "Self-development is the ontic foundation of Christ-development". Chapters 5-9 are intended to show the correctness of this statement.

3. The process of individuation as understood by Jung is directed entirely to happenings within the soul, nevertheless its practical application brings it into touch with the outside world. Many spiritual problems can only be solved in the context of society, by meeting and dealing with the problems which come from outside. Theoretically, however, the Jungian position is restricted to the interior sphere of the soul. Jung says that he is a scientist, whose "only means of knowledge is the experience"[1] which the soul affords the psychologist. All his utterances refer, therefore, merely to psychic facts and as a responsible scientist he cannot exceed this limit. According to Jung himself the philosophical pre-supposition of this position is Kant's epistemological statement on the unknowableness of metaphysical objects,[2] the "theory of the limitation and interiority of the spiritual".[3]

Philipp Lersch has laid bare the habits of thought which led to the imprisonment of the psychic in the cage of subjectivity and the denial to it of any transcendence to the outside world; he has traced the philosophical roots of this attitude back to Descartes whose theory of the two substances, the *res extensa* and *res cogitans*, tore them apart ontologically and isolated them one from the other.[4] Ever since, the soul and the world have been separated by a yawning gap. Psychology was only

[1] *Merkur* IV (1952), p. 469.
[2] Cf. Goldbrunner, *Individuation.*
[3] Philipp Lersch, *Seele und Welt: zur Frage nach der Eigenart des Seelischen*, Leipzig, 1943.
[4] *loc. cit.*, p. 40.

able to make statements about the spiritual sphere within; the soul became "world-less".

But, according to Lersch, the psychological view of phenomena itself breaks through the circle of subjectivity. Feelings such as pity evince a direct encounter with the Thou.[1] Love is a process of being affected by supra-subjective contents, it is a summons "in which we experience an ontically given relationship between the lover and the loved".[2] These feelings (pity, love, and also aesthetic experience) cannot be explained as purely interior and subjective phenomena. Wishing also produces actions which are the "clear expression of an actual transcendence of the aspiring soul".[3]

We are therefore on the threshold of a new "anthropological era" in which the gulf between the soul and the world is being closed psychologically. It is part of the very nature of the soul to stand in direct relationship to the world, to be affected by it and encounter it. The soul and the world are "two ontic spheres" which represent a "bi-polar, co-existent unity".[4] The soul can only be understood in relation to the world which it encounters. It belongs to the "reality of the soul" to be "in the world", in the sense in which Heidegger[5] uses the phrase.

According to this development in psychology the soul is defined essentially as a being "which is able to become aware of the world and therefore to encounter another being which does not belong to

[1] loc. cit., p. 18f. [2] loc. cit., p. 23. [3] loc. cit., p. 28.
[4] loc. cit., p. 41.   [5] See above, p. 25.

its own being but represents something quite different."[1]

For the soul the encounter with the world is not only a "stimulus" but a "call". Its self-realization does not take place only in the interior sphere; on the contrary, it only achieves authenticity by entering into relationship with the world.[2] In this way the two long separated endeavours of the human spirit are coming together again: philosophical-anthropological research on the one hand and ontic-experiential investigations on the other.

We owe a great debt to Ludwig Binswanger, Viktor Frankl, von Gebsattel, Ernst Michel, Ernst Trüb, Medard Boss, for having applied to depth psychology the new anthropology based on Heidegger's philosophy.[3]

When the process of individuation is set within the framework of this ontology the process itself is affected in three ways.

---

[1] *loc. cit.*, p. 41.

[2] "I come to my existence only by participation in the world ... Self-being is only real insofar as it appears in the objectivity of world-being." Karl Jaspers, *Philosophie*, II, *Existenzerhellung*, p. 48.

[3] Ludwig Binswanger,"Die daseinsanalytische Forschungsrichtung in der Psychiatrie" in *Schweiz. Archiv für Neurologie und Psychiatrie*, Vol. 57, pp. 210-223. Viktor Frankl, *Ärztliche Seelsorge*, Vienna, 1946; *Der unbewusste Gott*, Vienna, 1948; *Logos und Existenz*, Vienna, 1951. Viktor Emil von Gebsattel, *Christentum und Humanismus*, Stuttgart, 1947. Ernst Michel, *Rettung und Erneuerung des personalen Lebens*, Frankfurt, 1951. Ernst Trüb, *Heilung aus der Begegnung*, Stuttgart, 1951. Medard Boss, "Vom Weg und Ziel der tiefenpsychologischen Therapie, in *Psyche* I, 1948.

(a)   The soul is no longer "world-less", it is at home in the world and for its self-realization it looks not merely to the process in the interior sphere and the integration of consciousness and the unconscious, but also to the integration of itself and the world; i.e. action is required if it is to become itself. Decision within and action without both form part of the basic structure of existence. Together they require the complete devotion of the person.

Only when the truth heard within is "acted upon", can it exert its full influence. It is preceded by a "pale and unreal-seeming knowledge which only now appears in its full depth". Man grows together with this truth, he is stamped by it, he not only knows the truth, he is the truth. Man becomes "one with the deed of self-realization"[1]. This leads to a new kind of truth, namely, "existential truth".[2] Individuation leads to existential truth. This is of great significance in the sphere of religious education. Only the religious truth which is also "acted upon" can achieve its full power and be "realized". Whoever lives according to the words of Christ, will know their truth ("if any man will do his will he shall know of the doctrine").[3]

[1] Augustine speaks of the "doing of the truth" (*Conf.* X, 1) which binds man to the truth. Schmaltz makes full use of Augustine's idea for the individuation of man.

[2] Needless to say, there is a danger of over-emphasizing the "existential truth" and of its thereby becoming a mere individual truth.

[3] Cf. John 7, 17; 1 Cor. 4, 20: "It is power that builds up the kingdom of God, not words." Gal. 5, 6: "The

35

The unity of faith and life, the striving after existential truth in the process of individuation, leads to the realization of faith.

(b) The actuation of the person depends on the existence of other persons. The person needs to be in relationship with a Thou in order to come to itself; it can find its true nature only in dialogue.[1] Personal relationships become scientifically "legitimate" when the barrier between the soul and the world has been removed.[2]

The "dual mode of being" (Binswanger) of the person is part of the basic structure of human existence. "A man cannot become a personal man unless he responds to the call of the world around him" (Michel).

Individuation must therefore, *pace* Jung, take a new theoretical turning.[3] The Thou-relationship must not merely be set alongside the "self-entanglement" in which, according to Jung, it is imprisoned, but insofar as self-discovery is identical with the actuating of the person—personal encounter must become the most essential task on the way to the self; furthermore, the ultimate reality of the person is only awakened by the encounter with the absolute Thou, the person of

---

faith that finds its expression in love". *Imitation of Christ*, I, 1: "Whoever will fully understand and taste the words of Christ must endeavour to shape his whole life in the likeness of Christ."

[1] See above, p. 15.

[2] See above, p.26.

[3] This naturally has practical results which we shall discuss later on.

God. The self which Jung regards as "neuter" reveals its personal content and recognizes its Thou-character when the divine person calls it by its full name. The self acquires a name[1]. Personality is replaced by significance.[2] "The ground of man's being as a person is the dialogical relationship to transcendence; or to put it more precisely: the relationship to the Almighty who calls on the person by name".[3]

(c) Depth psychology constantly comes upon situations which are described as the "confluence" of the intellectual, spiritual, biological and physical strata. Spiritual and intellectual elements appear in the physical (in symptoms of disease too) and the physical draws the spiritual into dependence on itself. Contrary to his own philosophical presuppositions (psychology was for him a scientific discipline as it still is for Jung), Sigmund Freud and the whole psycho-therapeutic movement paved the way for the overcoming of the barrier between the body and the soul. It is impossible to understand or cure a neurosis with physical symptoms if the theory of the pure interiority of the soul is maintained. The practical experience of depth psychology coincides, therefore, with the new, yet age-old discovery of existential philosophy which sees the soul and the world in their togetherness

[1] See Chapter 9 on "Significance" below, p. 85.
[2] The concept of the personality will be avoided in what follows so as to escape the taint which it has acquired. It may also lead to an escape from significance. See above, p. 16.
[3] Michel, *loc. cit.*, p. 67.

and original unity.[1] But the result is that the body again acquires a logical place in psychology. Man not only has a body, he is body. It is by way of the body that the soul enters into communication with the world in space and time. The symbolic language of the body and the symbolism of nature[2] point to a line in the structure of human existence which crosses another line in the body, namely the line of man's individual history. The expression of the soul in the body (the incarnation of the spirit) and the historical, biographical mode of enquiry (long since used by psychotherapy in treatment of anamnesis—and also necessary in pastoral work when judging guilt and sin) are legitimate aids in education and psychagogy; they give the process of individuation a home in the here and now and demonstrate the "incarnation of the spirit and the spiritualization of the flesh".[3] In this context the soul is man's personal soul, the duty of which, however, is to realize the faith and it can do this only when incarnate in a body.

4. INDIVIDUATION

SINCE the life of the body is poorer than that of the spirit the incarnation of the spirit is never completely possible. There always remains a surplus which cannot be expressed in words and is there-

[1] See above, p. 33.   [2] See above, p. 15,
[3] Igor A. Caruso, *Psychoanalyse und Synthese der Existenz*, p. 229.

fore supra-objective;[1] August Brunner calls it the "supra-conscious". To it must be ascribed "the intelligent or, better, the wise direction of life which comes about without conscious deliberation yet is often more sensible than any direct effort; one might call it a spiritual instinct since, like an instinct, it does not need deductive thinking, it is the product of spiritual vision and direct experience". This "most active factor in man's spiritual life" is situated around the subjective centre of man; it is the core of the person which has to guarantee the unity of all the strata of the human being and its task is to incorporate all the strata in a personal outlook and mould them into a personal shape. Brunner concludes: "If this incorporation of all the strata in the high aims of the person is successful, for all his spirituality man will remain full of vitality and radiate an ever increasing human warmth and amiability".

The "supra-personal" and the self throw light on one another: both illuminate the relation between the person and individuation from a different standpoint; the supra-conscious in the dimension of that which lies above the strata, the self in the dimension of the inner sphere; and their task is clear: the permeation of all the strata of man with personal energies from above and from within and their incorporation in a personal outlook. The goal

[1] August Brunner, "Philosophisches zur Tiefenpsychologie und Psychotherapie", in *Stimmen der Zeit*, May, 1949. The "supra-conscious" has nothing to do with the Freudian conception of the "super-ego" which acts as an "unconscious censor".

of individuation is the "enthronement of the self" in the clear light of the supra-conscious. Four stages are involved:

1. I
2. Thou
3. We
4. God.

These are the four typical problems which life sets every man: 1. Authenticity of personal character; 2. Sex; 3. Community; 4. Religion. Dealing with them requires the employment of the conscious and unconscious spiritual energies which might be called the main organs of the human psyche and which must be shaped in a personal mould.

If one of these tasks which life sets us is evaded the spiritual organ will remain unawakened and undeveloped; it will escape from the rule of the self. Undifferentiated and uncultivated it will lead its own life in the unconscious and hinder the unity of human life. The longer this disturbance lasts the more set it will become and the more it will falsify the proper flow of the affects. And since each is dependent on the other in the psyche as in an organism the unhealthy attitude will influence the vital as well as the spiritual sphere of the soul and may ultimately result in a neurosis. This means that defective individuation, a failure to master one of the four typical problems, leaves man incompletely developed, changes his whole habitus and can even cause neurotic disease.[1] Is this not

[1] This is the point of departure for psychotherapy.

bound to have an influence on his religious life as well? Whereas the Christian formation of life is based on Matt. 5, 48: "you are to be perfect, as your heavenly Father is perfect" and the Christian striving after perfection is the basis of Christian ethics, depth psychology suggests that the striving for completeness should be set alongside the striving for perfection.[1] The man whose nature is in process of development, whose personal energy permeates all the strata of his being, is in a better position to follow the Gospel call to perfection than an "incomplete" person whose unconscious strata are leading a contrary life of their own because they have never been brought into relation with consciousness. Psychic completeness prepares man's energies for the responsible striving after perfection, it is the precondition on which their activity is based.

The Christian education of the self consists of two factors: the semi-conscious and semi-unconscious development of the plan which God has laid in every individual inasmuch as every individual represents a creative idea of God; and the equally conscious moulding of the self in accordance with the Gospel call to "be moulded into the image of his Son".[2] Nature and Grace-development and moulding—the two poles are for ever in a state of tension. Within this great context of the

[1] The concept of perfection, freed from restriction to the ethical, as it is used in the Sermon on the Mount, includes the concept of completeness.

[2] Rom. 8, 29; 2 Cor. 3, 18.

41

Christian education of the self, depth psychology points to a new polarity: completeness and perfection. In the age of spiritual levelling by collective forces psychic completeness acquires a new significance. Individuation as the process by which our nature achieves completeness (integration) often has a decisive influence on our whole way of life, since the realization of faith depends on it.

Individuation is related to the modern education for wholeness. "Culture as such always has in mind the whole man—or rather, the ideal, exalted man".[1] Individuation gives the educational endeavour to make man unified and complete, a new depth by its emphasis on psychic completeness.

The four stages of individuation, which are inseparably bound up together in real life, represent the scaffolding on which what follows is constructed.

5. THE RELATIVITY OF MAN'S RELATIONSHIP TO THE EXTERNAL WORLD

PSYCHIC completeness begins with the right functioning of the senses. Psychotherapy has discovered a remarkable situation in so-called "Freudism slips". It has discovered the psyche at work in the senses.[2] The ear does not receive

[1] Josef Sellmair, *Bildung in der Zeitenwende*, Würzburg, 1951.
[2] This is a very clear example of the contribution that psychotherapy is making to the new "anthropological era" discussed above (p. 33). In the positivistic era the senses were regarded merely as a complicated apparatus.

sounds and words like a microphone. It selects, though it is not the organ itself that selects but a censor in the psyche which often resides in the unconscious and which selects on the basis of repressed desires or dislikes and can, for example, cause the price for a certain article to be heard wrongly but in accordance with what the listener expected to hear. Hearing is therefore not only a physical process as it is when the hearing is done by a microphone but a complex of organic activity and the psyche. One might say that man with his problems is already contained in the process of hearing. And that could be shown to be true of all the senses. The eye does not see the right telephone number in the note-book because a repressed aversion to the impending conversation blinds the eye to the required number; or you discover at the railway station that you have left your purse at home and you cannot travel because you have no money to buy a ticket, thank God—as you now admit to yourself.[1]

The unconscious desire is contained in the listening, seeing and acting. The senses are not merely tools which man uses, they are not related to the world within, that world actually lives in the senses themselves. "It is impossible to construct a theory of seeing without taking into account the existence of man."[2]

[1] In his *Psychopathology of Everyday Life* in *Collected Works*, vol. 6, London, Freud gave a great number of examples of typical "Freudian slips".

[2] Romano Guardini, *Die Sinne und die religiöse Erkenntnis*, Würzburg, 1950, p. 23. "Looking is an

If this train of thought is continued it will be found that man's relation to the outside world does not work in the least independently like a machine, but is changed by the unconscious and semi-conscious and even by unconscious attitudes which do not in any way belong to the realm of disease but occur in the normal range of everyday life. A prejudice against a man which is accepted quite uncritically gives one a false impression of his features until the prejudice is dropped and "the scales fall from one's eyes". The results which follow from this discovery are of enormous significance in the realm of religion. If a man does not see and hear the outside world correctly, but in a distorted and imperfect fashion, coloured by his prejudices, he cannot do justice to his neighbour; he will not see the Church, the priest, the Gospel authentically and his religious life will be limited. Depth psychology points to various possible ways in which unconscious attitudes are formed which relativize the position of the I in the surrounding world.

1.   Professional life compels the soul to put on a uniform. For example, the teacher must pay constant attention to the effect he is having on a subordinate group. The teacher must always know more than the pupils. His task bestows authority and power upon him. The preponderance of the

---

activity which serves the will to life", Romano Guardini, *The Lord*, London, 1956.

person as teacher, applied to begin with at the right time and place, gradually becomes a habit and taken for granted. Power and authority are no longer merely granted to him to assist him in the function he has to perform: he himself personifies them. And all this begins to operate at the wrong time and place. The husband and father, the whole man acts like a teacher. He gradually begins to schoolmaster everything and everybody.

What has taken place here psychologically? The teaching profession represents a part which has to be played in front of the children as perfectly as possible. But instead of leaving his "uniform" at school and becoming a "civilian" again, instead of being the man Nature intends him to be, there is the danger that the teacher may identify himself with his role and become incapable of separating himself from it. He imputes to himself the power over children that was given to him for purely professional use. He reacts to every situation as a teacher and schoolmaster. He no longer knows that he is playing a role and always wearing a mask in front of his spiritual face. The mask inserts itself between his real nature and the world. He wears it in front of his face as the Greek actor wore the *persona* (mask) through which he spoke. Jung has called this intervening stratum the persona.[1] Thus we have the persona of the official, the clergyman, etc. The weaker a man's nature is, and the greater

---

[1] The psychological concept of the persona must be clearly distinguished from the philosophical concept of the person.

his personal vanity, the more he runs the danger of mistaking his persona for himself. He identifies himself with it. His character fails to develop in the round, it gets set in a groove. The vital energies of the soul are forced into a strait-jacket and fullness of life is rendered impossible. Anything that does not fit into the persona is repressed and slips back into the unconscious.

2. In education the persona of the teacher has an immediate effect on the environment. He will be incapable of helping the children to develop their own natures because he does not see the reality of the souls confided to him and fails to give them freedom to be individuals. He looks at everything through the spectacles of his persona and the very air about him is impregnated with his own desires and plans. Or a father may force his son into the profession which circumstances prevented him from entering himself, so that he can experience the fulfilment of his wishes after all. Such teachers and vain mothers and ambitious fathers force their children to lead an alien life, the life of the teacher, mother or father. The development of the child's own life is obstructed. Such children grow up with wishy-washy characters, lacking in freshness and immediacy. From their very childhood they have acquired foreign characteristics. A façade has been stuck on to them which acts as a persona and hides their own nature. Given a change of environment, however, the whole façade may be knocked down and the victim may

well then be completely "beside himself" as often happens when a child leaves a boarding school.

3. Public opinion is another factor in the formation of a persona. Every human being contains alien characteristics to the extent that he is dependent on public opinion. Unconsciously we conform to the things that are "done".[1] The anonymous, impersonal power of what "people" think and feel has a profound influence on our own thinking and feeling and willing and the more unconscious its influence the more comprehensive is its effect. This applies as much to an addiction to the latest fashion as to an exaggerated conservatism, which makes us do a thing in a certain way merely because "it has always been done this way". In both cases personal decision is left out of account altogether. Before it has had a chance of expressing its own view the soul has an attitude foisted upon it. It has no chance of "trying out" its own feelings. Public opinion acts like an air cushion between the soul and the world, preventing any real contact. It is true that the air cushion softens the impact, but it also lulls the self to sleep. The most valuable and intimate things in man—the person which has the capacity to make its own decisions—is asleep! Anyone who is never forced to make decisions and take risks is therefore never

[1] Cf. the significance of "other people" or "one" in Heidegger. The world of "other people" or "one" prevents man penetrating to his own existence. He is merely present but not existent.—See above p. 18.

able to "try himself out" and never reaches his own foundations at all. A pseudo-personality arises which seeks for its support not within itself but in the fluctuating public opinion of the outside world. Man sinks to the level of a collective being, he becomes a mass product, the willing organ of the anonymous power of public opinion.

4. The most dangerous formation of the persona proceeds from self-education. Observation shows that men accustom themselves to an automatic mode of reaction to the surrounding world, the purpose of which is to hide their true nature and at the same time make a particular kind of impression on the world. The blending of their own purposes with what the world expects of them is used to form an ideal image of themselves and they strive increasingly to approach this ideal, cultivating whatever accords with it and turning aside whatever is unsuitable. Both motives are quite legitimate since social and communal life would be impossible if everyone appeared in the shape of a raw product of nature and paid no heed to convention and custom. The thing becomes dangerous only when, in order to attain the "ideal", inferior qualities are not only hidden but repressed. To what extent it is possible to succumb to self-deception is shown by the fact that many people are disappointed when they hear their own voice and manner of speaking on the radio. The wish to make a particular impression on other people has prevented them from hearing their own voice

correctly.[1] The same experience may be shattering when one watches oneself or someone else moving from one milieu to another, from professional to private life, or in intercourse with people of different social standing, with superiors or subordinates. The change is not made consciously for reasons of prudence. What has happened is that an unconscious change in behaviour has become part of one's flesh and blood, and is therefore beyond control. An isolating stratum—the ideal image —has inserted itself between the world and the self.

The danger of the persona formed by self-education lies still deeper, however. Whence does the man who is striving to attain the "ideal image" of himself derive the assurance that his self-made ideal corresponds to the idea which is planted within him and which God had of him when he was created? A self-conceived ideal can endanger the development of his whole nature. The natural growth of the individual cannot be determined or calculated in advance. Ignaz Klug has drawn attention to the immanent development within us in these words: "In a single case everyone can act or fail to act or act differently. But when a whole series of actions is involved, how does the matter stand then? Does not experience show that all our actions spring ultimately from the immutable depths of our being? ... as a whole they always

[1] Even if the difference between the sound heard from within and the sound heard from without is taken into account.

follow the laws of the inner structure".[1] If as a result of the striving after a false ideal a persona is formed which contradicts the inner structural laws and the depths of the being, a schism will be formed which will be felt to be lacking in authenticity from outside but which will have a destructive influence within. Such a man will live contrary to his own nature and fail to achieve his own nature.

The result is the unauthenticity of a psyche which is hidden by the persona: fullness of life is made impossible, an alien life is lived instead of a life of one's own, personal decisions are evaded, one's own nature frustrated. The discrepancy between outer and inner, between persona and true nature, between appearance and content makes this kind of person unauthentic. The consequences appear externally as well as internally. The relationship of the person to the outside world is distorted; the I and the reality of the outer world are separated by a medium in passing through which all the rays undergo refraction as when light rays pass through water. The persona distorts family relationships and is often the cause of quarrels which are regretted and admitted but which are repeated again and again because the root causes have not been removed. There are difficulties in social life, with professional colleagues, neighbours, in church life, and with superiors. In spite of deliberate effort relationships with neighbours remain inexplicably ill-starred.

[1] Ignaz Klug, *Tiefen der Seele*, Paderborn, 1940, p. 62.

The reason is that all the man's human relationships are stamped with an ideal that does not correspond to reality. All external relationships are tainted by the persona.

Behind all these symptoms there is a fact of general significance: psychic things influence a person's relationship to the external world. This relationship is by no means a given fact like the distance between two houses; it is relative and dependent on spiritual attitudes; it depends on whether inner falsity leads to the formation of a persona or whether man stands in the truth. Fundamentally, therefore, every man's conception or image of the world is a subjective "projection of the world".[1] How greatly a "projection of the world" distorted by a persona can stand in the way of a Christian view of the world and the realization of faith![2] Conversely, faith influences the senses by way of the soul.

The soul's commitment to the truth purifies the senses and gives them their full power. The state of faith makes it possible to look reality in the eye. To the extent that man has a faith that is real, the relativity of a subjective view of the world yields to a vision of the reality of the world as redeemed creation. Faith penetrates the senses and human relationships just as really and imperceptibly as the persona inhibits the senses. Imperceptibly the Christian comes to see the world as it really is and

[1] Cf. Medard Boss, "Vom Weg und Ziel der tiefenpsychologischen Therapie", *Psyche* I, 1948, pp. 321-339.
[2] "Faith is a capacity for seeing"—Romano Guardini.

he is empowered to judge it aright;[1] and this in its turn confirms his faith. There is a mutual connection between the realization of faith and liberation from a persona. How greatly they condition one another can be seen in the influence of the persona on the inner life. A man who is hidden behind a persona does not live his own life, he is determined from without, instead of living, he is lived. He does not make his own decisions and insofar as he does not realize his own nature, he does not live from himself. He does not wholly exist, he is not existent, to use the terminology of the existentialists. He does not take hold of his own existence; he misses his own true nature. A persona therefore influences the very core of the person. It prevents the actuating of the person, genuine personal encounters with other men and with God become more or less impossible. A man with a persona can, admittedly, have a religion, but it cannot be his religion; it is bound to be a sham. It will seem a sham to others too and therefore be incapable of bearing a true witness. The realization of faith presupposes existence and the persona makes existence impossible.

6. AUTHENTICITY

MANY people can only be helped spiritually if they can be brought to an understanding of their

---

[1] I Cor. 2, 15: "The man who has spiritual gifts can scrutinize everything, without being subject, himself, to any other man's scrutiny".

persona and enabled to separate themselves from it. The next steps on the road to authenticity are then the gradual dissolution of the persona and growing into a form of life which is authentic and representative of the person's true nature. There are great difficulties here. The persona is like a house in which the soul has made itself at home. All the rooms evince the spirit of subjective desires and ideals. The intellect is constricted within the thought patterns of the persona; genuine feelings have been stifled by the acquired patterns of behaviour; the senses have become the servants of the "false" ego. Man stands in his own way; and all too often he regards his "trouble" as his good fortune. He is separated from reality in a state of isolation of which he is himself quite unaware. Three factors must work together to penetrate the prison of the persona.[1]

1.   What is the spiritual adviser to appeal to if all the vital functions have been changed by the persona? Will not the "patient" laugh if he is told that he is not genuine, that his true nature is quite different? Will he grasp the point at all? Is there a tribunal within which he can still respond? It is here that the mystery of the person is revealed. It comes to the patient's aid by emitting signals which

[1] Though we are disregarding here the extreme cases of a persona which leads to neurosis, the persona must nevertheless be shown in an extreme form since the average case makes it impossible to see the phenomena clearly. Experience will, however, also reveal fragments and partial formations of a persona.

make the ego listen. Some word of criticism or correction gives him no peace. Painful though the impact of the word is, it is answered by a feeling of genuine liberation. The "patient" begins to suspect his previous opinions and ideas; or the reactions may be so strong that it seems as though the very supports of the house were being sawn away or the ground under his feet disappearing. Something inside him rises up against the hitherto existing I. On the one hand, traditional elements assert themselves: custom and habit, public opinion and prejudices, family pride and professional honour, ideals, vanity and fear. On the other side, however, there is a mysterious sense of an early morning freshness, a sense of the narrowness of the attitude to life that has hitherto been taken for granted and a sense of freedom, of the delightfulness of existence, of true being and of the impossibility of living in future without them. The ego begins to listen intently to a basic melody which is trying to sound in the soul and which is telling him what he was really intended to be. In clashes with the world in which such selfish passions as indignation, anger, irritation, pride and triumph are aroused, the idea occurs that one's weak spots are being affected and that the persona is the cause of the difficulties. To an ever increasing extent, repressed potentialities come to the surface which cause discomfort because they confuse and yet allure.[1] Slowly a point is formed which confronts the ego and defends

[1] Psychotherapy introduced the term "shadow" for this.

with increasing assurance its claim to be the true ego, the other one being a mere persona. For a time the "patient" does not really know who he is, on which side he is to take his stand, whether the ego should dwell in the old persona or in the new awareness of life. This insecurity and uncertainty shows how closely identified the ego is with the pseudo-personality of the persona and the time it takes to become detached from it. Despite the seriousness of the situation the important moments in this process are like a game which can be only too easily upset by any outside influence. Only when the powers of consciousness, above all, the intellect, are released in the to and fro of the game will the interaction of rational and irrational factors produce a true result. Suddenly, one does not quite know how, the game is over and the ego emerges with a new and determined sense of direction; the true nature of the man has at last succeeded in breaking through the persona.

All this is the veil which hides the mystery described by such expressions as: determination and freedom; uncertainty and venture; natural growth and personal decision; confidence in nature and the guidance of grace. The discovery of the ego is a vital beginning in the soul which cannot be explained in rational terms. It is the mysterious result of the confluence of the unconscious, the conscious and supra-conscious. But whence comes this mysterious drive from the depths of the soul, this urge for authenticity on which everything depends? And what is it that turns the scale in the decisive and momentous battle? It is the core of the person or, psychologically speaking, the self that decides the issue. We are faced here with the mystery of the spirit that is capable of self-determination. Whether the persona is superseded depends on the strength of the power and appeal of the self. This impulse from the soul within, in which rational and irrational elements are intermingled "irrationally", is a criterion of the personal strength of a man.

2.   The helper, be he priest or teacher, occupies an odd position in this spiritual conversation with a patient suffering from a persona. He speaks with the "patient" face to face, but through him, into the heart and core of the person. He realizes that his partner in this conversation about the things of the persona often does not and cannot understand him, but he appeals to the person that is asleep behind the persona. It is not the spiritual adviser's words that are important so much as the mysterious carrying power of his words. It is often not the deliberately intended word that strikes the depths but, as is later admitted, a seemingly insignificant remark. The important thing is that the words should possess an energy which bestows on them the force of an appeal. The person of the speaker should evoke the core of the person in the other. The best helper will be the person who has already come completely to himself. Person is resonant to person.[1] The existence of one person calls the

[1] See Chapter 8, section 3, pp. 80 ff.

other person to take hold of his existence; wakes, calls and lures.

The ability to help on the depth-psychological level is dependent, therefore, on the fulfilment of one great precondition: the personal existence of the adviser. Mere knowledge of the circumstances is not enough since it is a matter of changes which occur at a level too deep for the mere intellect to grasp. Someone has written, "I knew about all that long ago, but was unable to realize it until what was happening in me was revealed in conversation with another. Since then I have been different."[1]

3. The two factors that have been mentioned—the personal strength of the "patient" and the personal existence of the adviser—will be fruitless without, as the third factor, the appropriate situation. In psychotherapy the situation is created by the suffering perceived in the neurosis. In the average case which comes to the attention of the priest the situation only emerges within the framework of a long development. It is possible for the conversation to return repeatedly to the same point and it may be only on the fourth occasion that the appropriate situation presents itself. Even if it is possible to list a few preliminary requirements for the creation of the right situation—the preparatory awakening to the problems of self-discovery; being frightened by imposing circum-

[1] See also Chapter 13 on "The religious conversation", pp. 120 ff.

stances; a favourable time and the necessary quiet for the conversation—it is nevertheless impossible to create the situation deliberately. It is the place where the personal guidance of a man by Grace is revealed. It is not unlike "conversion" and indeed the liberation from a persona and the process of conversion are often bound up with one another.

The helper finds himself here within a texture of the most subtle, invisible relationships of a human and supernatural kind. Insofar as he has laid aside all self-seeking and become utterly receptive to the other person he can be used as a "catalyst".[1] The art of spiritual advice and every form of human guidance consists for the most part in an ability to tune into the other's wavelength; in other words, to love him objectively. Retrospectively the adviser will be able to see whether he himself is free of all remains of the persona.

Step by step differentiation from the persona leads to complete detachment from it. The discrepancy between inner and outer is slowly evened out. At the same time the sense of the authentic way of life best suited to one's own nature increases. As the process of individuation advances, so the appropriate mode of life will become clearer. Self-discovery alone makes possible a life in which there is no identification with a persona. Some teachers are a good example of this. They

[1] The disadvantage of the chemical metaphor is that in conversation the results are of a purely personal nature, not scientifically ascertainable.

act on their pupils by the sheer maturity of their humanity and they have hardly any disciplinary troubles at all, although they control their classes with a very light rein.

7.   THE ENCOUNTER

SEXUAL encounters play an important part in the actuating of the person.[1] Metaphysically the person is related to a Thou,[2] its very nature is to be in dialogue. An essential stage in the maturing process is fulfilled in the psychic happenings which occur in and around sexual encounters and they have a part to play in preparing the person for its encounter with God himself.

These encounters awaken and release the personal in man though through a sphere of spiritual life which is set like a rind around the core of the person. The capacity for love[3] is the necessary passage leading to the core of the person or, if it is wrongly used or not used at all, a strait-jacket. The capacity for love is waiting to be used and moulded by the person, for its purpose is to find fulfilment as a personal mode of expression.

[1] "It has been shown that the person is actuated in the I-Thou situation but does not arise from it"—Romano Guardini, *Welt und Person,* p. 154. The term "encounter" will be always used here to mean "sexual encounter" since it represents the "encounter" *par excellence.*

[2] See above, p. 15.

[3] Cf. the diagram in Goldbrunner, *Individuation,* Notre Dame, 1964, p. 124.

This second stage in the process of individuation, from the I to the Thou, arouses a mass of feelings and capacities which penetrate consciousness from the unconscious. They have to be dealt with individually, to be set in order and seen as a whole. As the intellectual permeation of all these strata advances they submit to the guidance of the self. In the truth about love there are many strata[1] and completeness will be achieved only by those who have the courage to see and accept all the strata.

1. The biological approach only covers the mating and reproductive instincts. This stratum of love which we call *Sex* corresponds to the part of the soul which is related to the sexual aspect of the body. It is the teacher's task to ease the way for the awakening of the sexual instinct in puberty by objective and gradual enlightenment and to assist

[1] Consider the number of possible answers to the question "What is a pearl?" The chemist replies that it is a carbon compound; the biologist will report that it arises from a diseased excrescence of the mussel; for the merchant the pearl is a precious object of merchandise and for the lady it is an ornament; but the poet speaks of the pearl as the "tear of the sea". Naturally they are all right since the truth about the pearl has many different strata and embraces all the replies. It would not be doing justice to the pearl to leave out one particular layer of the truth, for example, the chemical or biological stratum, on the grounds that that particular aspect of the truth is brutal. In the same way the truth about love has many strata and when we ask "what is love?" we should not omit to take note of the replies of the biologist, the philosopher, the theologian and—last but not least—the depth psychologist.

its incorporation in a Christian way of life. Instruction in the biological facts should continue until the young person is ripe for marriage. Any uncertainty prevents Sexus from being permeated by the whole person. "Christian asceticism must bear in mind that in spite of his evil inclinations man is in order so long as he feels his instincts along with bad tendencies and takes them up into his suffering. This suffering serves to preserve his physical as well as spiritual health."[1] In other words, in every encounter between the sexes, Sexus will be present as a basic current, on or below the surface, consciously or unconsciously. The result is that there can be no such thing as a "Platonic friendship" between young, maturing people of different sexes; all such relationships must be regarded as love relationships and treated accordingly.[2]

2.   On the border line between *Sexus* and *Eros* a law comes into operation which pervades the whole cosmos; the law of attraction and repulsion, of sympathy and antipathy. It operates in the mineral world, it is the reason why some plants fail to thrive side by side and it separates and unites animals. Human beings[3] are also subject to its spell and they sense it more or less clearly as an "atmosphere". The more clearly one is consciously aware of the rising and falling of this barometer

[1] H. E. Hengstenberg, *Christliche Askese*, Regensburg, 1936, p. 93.
[2] See below, p. 64 and pp. 67 ff.
[3] Cf. Goethe's *Wahlverwandtschaften* (Elective affinities).

61

the better able one will be to solve the problems set by this law: sympathy and antipathy must be subjected to objective criteria in the life of human society. Within the framework of sexual encounters this involuntary reaction to the other person mediates between *Sexus* and *Eros:* if such an encounter is to be permanently established in marriage and family life this factor must be examined with all the greater care, because it will determine the emotional level of married life.[1]

3. To make this clear it is necessary to consider the problem in the context of the human capacity for love which finds expression in the number of different forms or categories. In every form of love there are two basic elements: a tendency towards union and sharing (*intentio unitiva*) and a tendency towards devotion (*intentio benevolentiae*). The different parts they play leave their mark on the form the particular relationship assumes.

In parental love the two "intentions" hold the balance at the outset. The parents form a unity with the child, a unity in the nestling warmth of

[1] Three points seem to be a precondition for marriage:

1. Agreement of the partners on the ultimate questions of life.

2. The same level of values (cultural and intellectual).

3. The same level of emotional life.

The psychotherapist hears about a great deal of marital suffering which results from the neglect of these preconditions. The many sexual neuroses show how little guidance there is in the problem of incorporating the energy of love in the conduct of daily life.

which the child thrives, for it cannot exist on its own. The parents surround it with the gifts of the *intentio benevolentiae*. As the child grows, however, and becomes more independent and more detached from its parents, the *intentio benevolentiae* should recede into the background. To give up the children requires an act of renunciation on the part of the parents which often causes heart-break.[1] "This readiness to give up their children is profoundly characteristic of parental love."[2] The *intentio benevolentiae* should strive to set the child more and more on its own feet and make the parents more and more superfluous. The child is being educated for life and should be helped to make its entry into adult life. Once the child has left home both the "intentions" are reduced to the function of merely helping when the occasion requires. In old age the capacity for *intentio benevolentiae* declines and the *intentio unitiva* looks rather to the child to provide comfort for its parents in the evening of life.

In the child's love the *intentio unitiva* predominates to begin with. The child feeds on its parents. The tendency to try and bring happiness to its parents remains in the background but as the years pass this *intentio benevolentiae* gradually replaces the *intentio unitiva* and the child strives to

[1] If a mother does not release her daughter, for example, she hinders the child's growth to maturity and this can influence the child's professional and even religious life as well as the purely physical.

[2] Cf. D. von Hildebrand, *Metaphysik der Gemeinschaft*, pp. 51-86.

serve its parents in a spirit of gratitude and love. If the ageing parents are taken into the child's own home the two intentions will balance one another.

In the love of friends both partners in the relationship stand as it were hand in hand facing the values with which they want to enrich one another. The intention is a limited union, not a complete union but "an understanding association with one another". (Hildebrand.)

In the love of the betrothed the lovers take hold of each other's hands and give themselves to one another. In this relationship the *intentio unitiva* and the *intentio benevolentiae* are blended together. This kind of love is marked by what Hildebrand describes as a "total awareness of a special quality" in which a unique capacity for seeing the other is developed. The theme of this love is the beloved himself; it arouses the innermost essence of the person. All the protective guards of objectivity are dropped and, defenceless, the ego confronts the Thou. In this contemplation of each other's nature there is, as Hildebrand says, "participation in the other's being which is incomparably more profound than that which is possible in the material world".

Neighbourly love is of all the various kinds of love the one that aims least of all at awakening a response in the other, for the other person does not stand within the gaze of love as an individual but as a creature made in the image of God, as one who possesses an immortal soul which has been redeemed with the blood of Christ. The *intentio benevolentiae* is clearly predominant. "It hastens," writes Hildebrand, "to the other, in the fullest sense, but not to be united with him but rather to cover him with goodness". It sees the other person *in conspectu Dei*. The neighbour is not simply "material for the exercise of charity". He is seen as God sees him. From the standpoint of religious education the combination of the love of friends and the love of the betrothed is particularly interesting since this hybrid form of love is often a problem in adolescence. In encounters with the opposite sex *Eros* oscillates uncertainly between friendship and sexual love and a dividing line has to be established. What has then to be decided is whether it would be right to convert the encounter into married life and a family or whether justice will be done if the meeting has a beginning, a climax and also an end: whether it should become permanent or remain only temporary.

4. For the realization of faith it is of great importance whether *Eros* and religion, the capacity for love and the relationship with God, are separate and hostile to one another or whether a synthesis is arrived at in which they can further one another.

Eros and religion are dependent on one another. Whoever separates them and sows enmity between them creates a division between love for man and love for God. Where *Eros* and religion are mutually exclusive *Eros* becomes vulgar and religion cold. *Eros* sinks to the level of animal lust and religion is lifeless. For it is *Eros* that loosens the ground of the soul, making it soft and malleable. It cultivates the powers of enthusiasm without which the religious life grows weary. Where, on the other hand, *Eros* and religion are combined, *Eros* is ennobled, and spiritualized and gives religion vitality. Both have much in common and ought to work hand in hand. They have the same mortal enemy: self-love. Both are trying to attain the same goal: redemption from the ego, out of isolation into communion. But there is a difference between *Eros* and religion, not in the sense of a rivalry or antithesis but in the fact that *Eros* stops half-way and only leaves a mere premonition of the meaning of redemption. But even though *Eros* cannot bring complete fulfilment the part of the way which it can travel must and can be rooted in religion. It points back to the days of Creation, as Franz Xaver Arnold has said:[1] "Sexual pleasure in marriage must be seen as the God-willed creative joy of those who continue and complete the work of the Creator according to his own plan". And *Eros* also points forward to the Kingdom of God at the end of time since the parables of the heavenly wedding feast suggest that those who wed should understand something of the *Eschata*. And all this implies that *Eros* has been created with God as its ultimate goal.

5. Once the positive religious content of *Eros* has been established it is possible, without defaming it, to accept the grave term *"Eros thanatos"*.[2]

[1] "Das eheliche Geheimnis in Theologie und Seelsorge", *Universitas* II, October, 1947, p. 1155. Cf. *Man and Woman*, New York, 1963.

[2] J. Bernhart, *De Profundis,* Leipzig, 1939, p. 129 f.

"It does not die, but it is always dying." It blossoms and unites human beings; but it also fades and dies; it blossoms again only to fade once more; it is a "being of death". It is unable to sustain a human relationship over long periods of time unless it is supported by other forces, the forces of loyalty and trust. This means that it is important that those who succumb to *Eros* should realize what has happened and be able to release themselves from its hold. *Eros* is not the driver but only one of the horses which draw the vehicle of the soul. It can provide access to a person, it can awaken a person but the person must be able to rise above it.

6. This is where depth psychology comes in. By means of its concept of "projection" it can help those who have succumbed to *Eros* to differentiate themselves from it and set it in its rightful place.

Once the condition of being in love is taken seriously it is possible to show the "mechanism" of projection at work. The lovers see one another in a radiance which outshines and often conceals their own often insignificant reality. They see one another as they are "really intended to be", in the perfection of an original Idea of Creation, which is why their mutual fascination has a religious feeling about it, until one or other of them is disillusioned by some occurrence or by the banality of everyday life, and the magic vanishes. The other then asks, as if waking from a dream: "Was I blind? What did I really see? He (or she) is in fact quite different after all." This experience helps towards a realization that when people are in love they do not see the reality of each other. They project on to the beloved something from their own psyche. This something remains over as the sum of all the contents and qualities of the other when the reality of the beloved is subtracted from the total image that the lover has conceived;[1] it represents the ideal partner of whom the actual partner may only represent a small fraction. Blind *Eros* has been concentrated in an unconscious picture of the beloved. Depth psychology calls the image that is projected on to the partner the *anima* (in the case of the male) and the *animus* (in that of the female). Both are archetypes of the unconscious.[2] They form an autonomous complex which can produce a new projection at any time whenever someone of the opposite sex appears in whom there is something corresponding to the archetype. The anima or animus then becomes virulent, fills the whole household of the soul with its atmosphere, surges through consciousness with an abundance of pleasurable sensations, permeates the mind and all the senses. The senses are filled with subjective contents which dominate the relationship between the two persons. The relationship is pre-personal because it is determined by the mechanism of projection. It is impossible for the two to make a free decision since they have succumbed to an urge compounded of *Eros* and *Sexus*. So long as the

[1] C. G. Jung, *Archetypes of the Collective Unconscious* in *Collected Works*, vol. 9, London, 1958.
[2] See Goldbrunner, *Individuation*, London, 1956.

projection continues in force no personal relationship is feasible. Greatly though being in love can awaken the capacity for true meeting it can also act as a hindrance if it is uncontrolled. To be overwhelmed by a projection is tantamount to being enslaved to *Eros*. The problem is to differentiate the ego from *Eros* which is only one part of the soul.

It is no use rehearsing to oneself the facts of a projection with the mind alone. The spiritual reality in the senses is so strong and the appearance so captivating[1] that there is a danger of the relationship being made concrete. The person caught up in a projection is like the king's son in the fairy story who is travelling to the castle on the other side of the deep forest where the precious stone or elixir of life is awaiting him. The journey through the impenetrable forest—the land of love—is full of dangers and adventures. Like many of his predecessors he will be turned into stone if he fails to solve the problems set him, if, for example, he speaks prematurely or "takes food", i.e. indulges in premature sexual pleasures; or for fear of the transforming circle of fire (the fire of love that glows in the heart) falls back. The story is a warning—clothed in the metaphorical language of the unconscious—and vividly describes the effect on the process of maturing when the capacity for love is not related to and shaped by the whole person.

[1] When a primitive man goes to a cinema for the first time he considers the happenings on the screen as real. He only loses the illusion when he has himself switched the projection apparatus on and off a few times and discovers the little picture hidden in the machine.

An understanding of the mechanism of projection has to be acquired by observing the law of encounter which forbids a consummation of the sexual relationship. The restraint that this enforces makes it possible for the anima to become fully conscious and also for it slowly to recede. Its power of the senses gradually diminishes and at the end of the encounter there is a grateful awareness of the service which the other person has performed. Oppressive though a new encounter may be, the soul now has knowledge, based on actual experience, of the possibility of projection and the intermingling of anima and reality and it strives cautiously to distinguish the reality of the new partner from the projected radiance. Insofar as this differentiation is successful, insight into the person of the other will grow and the way will be free for a truly personal relationship. It will then be possible to decide soberly whether both partners are mutually suited for a life together when *"Eros thanatos"* has withered and is silent. The "objectivation" of the anima[1] must take place before a mere encounter can be transferred, in a responsible spirit on both sides, to a life of marriage and the rearing of a family.

The modes of encounter are of many kinds. They range from silent admiration from a distance[2] to the temptation of the "adventure of love". Endur-

[1] C. G. Jung, *Two Essays in Analytical Psychology* in *Collected Works*, Vol. 7, London, 1954. Cf. also Goldbrunner, *Individuation*.

[2] The cultural activities of literature, drama and the fine arts are effective in the same direction.

ance in any encounter between the sexes requires discipline, self-control and the most scrupulous honesty with oneself. It often involves most painful spiritual struggles but these are the price that has to be paid for growing into maturity.[1]

The positive reward is the spiritual permeation and conquest of the capacity for sexual love. The anima is linked to consciousness. The Ego expands inwardly and is sustained by an inner feeling that is expressed in a divination of the breadth and depth of the soul, of its brightness and darkness. The anima embodies all the dark, soft, receptive side of the soul. This whole area of the soul is now linked and "yoked" to consciousness. The feminine unconscious is united to the masculine consciousness. A person who is striving to attain completeness in this way gives the impression of being "inspired", which is why Jung introduced the term "anima" for this part of the soul. If, however, the anima is excluded from consciousness, for example, by repression or evasion, it gives the impression of being "soulless".[2]

A second result of the objectivation of the anima is the synthesis of consciousness and the unconscious

[1] If an encounter can take place within the framework of a community with a definite shape it will be helped and protected by that community even when in danger.
[2] "After the middle of life constant loss of the anima means an increasingly serious loss of vitality, flexibility and humanity", C. G. Jung, *Archetypes of the Collective Unconscious* in *Collected Works*, Vol. 9, Part I, London, 1958. Contrary to the medieval view, Jung believes, therefore, that the sexual is important not merely for the reproduction of life but for the whole life of the person.

which is thus prepared. A middle element is formed between the two poles which are in vital tension and this emerges as a balancing and directing force, as a new depth within the Ego or as a new force confronting the Ego. This invisible and secret counsellor may be compared to the "political sense". The ruler who has conquered and reconnoitered a new province will take the new area into account in all his decisions, since the whole of his kingdom is a living organism. His political acumen will help him to decide what is best for the whole. In just the same way this third element represents the synthesis between the two halves of the soul. This third element is the self. To the extent that the first and second stages in the process of individuation have been achieved man begins to live from the centre of the "self", or, since the self is identical with the core of the person, the actuating of the person is completed; it becomes capable of personal encounters.[1] The other party in the encounter calls to the person through the anima, rousing and claiming it for the Thou, thus providing a preliminary exercise for the encounter with God.

8. CREATURELINESS

THE third stage in the process of individuation confronts the person with new problems. In the

---

[1] The psychologism in depth psychology is not overcome by rejecting its positions but by their incorporation in the organization of the levels of being.

various forms of social life man meets others not as a Thou but as We; i.e. he is involved in social relationships inevitably and involuntarily. The sphere in which these relationships take place is different from that in which relationships with a Thou occur. We propose to discuss first of all the various forms of social relationship and their anthropological significance, then the archetypal organs attached to them and finally we shall try to show how the archetypal stratum can be penetrated so as to attain a personal approach to social relationships.

1. Man grows into the various classical forms of community during the course of his life. The purpose of the family is the moulding of parents, children and brothers and sisters into a community which thrives in an atmosphere of mutual love. All other communities are contained within the family in embryo. It is a cell which projects out into many spheres of culture and economy. As a community the family has what Hildebrand terms "metaphysical classicity". Hence its influence on man's self-realization is of the greatest importance.

The next larger form of community is the social or professional sphere in which man lives his life. It is formed wherever men have a sense of belonging together on geographical or historical grounds (e.g. common place of residence, common profession) though their sense of community with one another may be quite inarticulate. To begin with they come in contact with one another by force of outward circumstances (next-door neighbours, professional colleagues). The basis of the relationship is always a primitive mutual interest, a bare association from which, however, in certain situations, especially disaster or trouble, a sudden sense of solidarity may arise. In the case of the nation the emphasis is on an inter-personal atmosphere which, as Hildebrand points out, colours people's attitude "to various spheres in a special way", from the development of a particular attitude to life and a particular ethos to a certain psychic sense and a particular rhythm of life which influences even the construction of the sentence and the intonation of the language. The personified "genius of the nation" (e.g. Plato, Goethe, Beethoven) has a function rather like that of a medium; the individual feeds on these great figures. The nation forms a "total individuality" which determines the relationship between the individual and the community in many spheres.

The vital nerve of the State is the law. The elemental needs of life, public affairs (such as security) are its proper sphere. The State should create the framework for the nation. To this end it needs power and authority and the organs with which to execute the functions with which it is charged. The members of the State constitute as it were the objects of the life of the State. The State's tendency to annex more and more originally independent spheres (that of education in particular) and the collective responsibility for the position and policy of one's own State in relation to other States, force man into situations which promote his self-realization.

Humanity is a metaphysical community. Its sphere is man's ultimate destiny, his relationship to God and the world of ultimate values. Humanity is the great community in which men share their common destiny of birth and death. It is usually latent, hidden by other forms of community, but to experience it existentially adds a necessary depth to the development of the person.[1]

As a supernatural community the Church stands athwart all the forms so far enumerated. It is concerned with salvation, election and judgment. As the mystical Body of Christ the Church penetrates into the very core of the person.

All these forms of community can be so moulded as to be favourable or unfavourable to personal development. Such communal situations as eating and feasting together, accidents, catastrophes, illness and recovery, can also act in the same way, favourably or unfavourably to the growth of the person. If they are taken up into the service of personal life they will begin to "speak" and their "word" will be released.

2. The archetypes of the Father and Mother, Brother and Sister are constellated in the family. The psychotherapists were the first to recognize the significance of the child's early experiences of its parents. Paths are laid down and travelled in early childhood which it is difficult to change in

[1] See below, p. 84.

75

later life. The archetype of the Father is a pattern of experience which represents the male principle in the cosmos, the image of God the Father, the principle of authority and order. The archetype of the Mother illuminates everything female in the cosmos, representing home and security, hence the terms "Mother Church" and "Mother Earth". When the usual detachment of children from their parents takes place this involves the "objectivation" of the two archetypes. Both were projected on to the parents and developed unconsciously. If the usual process of detachment fails to take place, whether from fear of adult life on the child's part or possessiveness on the parents' part, the two archetypes are projected on to the choice of a mate. Unconsciously and unsuspectingly the man looks for his mother in his bride; the projection distorts his view of the partner's true reality. Similarly the girl looks for her father in her lover. In each case a "pseudo-existence" is constructed. The unconscious projections are a hindrance to personal reality.

The archetypes which are bound up with the everyday circle in which we live and move react similarly. The Neighbour, the Comrade, the professional Colleague as helper or rival, the Traitor, etc. The problem is to penetrate through the projection, for instance, of the Enemy in the shape of the professional competitor, to the reality. The conflict in one's own soul and with the outside world contributes to the process of individuation if the archetype with all its urges and energies is able to penetrate into consciousness, if it is mastered intellectually by not allowing oneself to be carried away by passions and by choosing one's moves deliberately and after due consideration.[1]

The archetype of the Nation which we should like to mention here is the "genius" which finds expression in artists, for example, and to which the individual can succumb. The fact that contacts between the nations are becoming more and more frequent and taken for granted means that devotion to national archetypes must now be limited. Mention must also be made of the archetypes of the Doctor and Priest, because they are so important.[2] In primitive times they belonged together since healing power was attributed to God alone. Healing and salvation were intermingled. Because of this connection between the doctor and the priest, which Christianity revived in the expected Saviour, a religious aura surrounds the doctor even to-day, just as, conversely, the priest is often expected to help in the natural rather than the supernatural sphere which is his true province.

It is important for the realization of faith to see the archetype of the Priest as the mediator between man and the *Eschata* in the strictly Christian sense. It is important to differentiate the human reality of the priest from his office, not least for the priest's own sake. We shall have more to say about this below.[3]

[1] See below, p. 83.
[2] Both also penetrate the spheres of other communities and the State. But they seem to be more related to the national community by reason of their function and their innermost nature.   [3] See below, pp. 120 ff.

The archetype of the King is bound up with the power of the State. Even when he appears to-day in civilian dress, the old image of the Ruler comes to mind. How virulent this archetype may become and condition a whole people is shown by the fervour of popular devotion to dictators. They themselves do all they can to attract to themselves a fascinating projection of the archetype. The maturity of a people can be measured by the degree to which it resists such projections.

The most inaccessible of all archetypes is the one represented by the experience of humanity. After all, it is comparatively seldom that the metaphysical situation of the human race bursts upon us at all and yet the mastery and control of all the social archetypes depends on their being set in relationship to the archetype which sustains them all: the archetype of the Brother or the Sister of the human race as such.

It should be the duty of the theatre to help. When an archetypal situation is shown on the stage, and the actor plays as it were with the archetypes of his audience—the audience are fascinated, moved, overwhelmed. The great playwright succeeds in breaking through the archetypal situation, revealing the projections and illuminating the background, showing men's ultimate relationship to one another in the community we call the human race, making plain the whole joy and misery of men as brothers one of another. Every reference to the archetype, whether it is experienced directly or merely spoken, is "moving", i.e. it awakens a stronger voice within us than our own. To speak in primeval images is to speak as with a thousand voices, to move and overwhelm, to raise what is described from a state of isolation and transitoriness into the sphere of the universal, to raise the purely personal destiny to the level of the human destiny in general, thereby releasing in all of us those helpful energies which have enabled humanity again and again to save itself from danger and disaster.[1] The theatre can have a purifying, deepening effect by working on the unconscious in man.[2] Consciousness resists to begin with. It feels that one's fellow men are a burden and a nuisance. And the objective uniqueness of every person seems to justify the feeling that it may even be degrading to have to reckon ourselves all members one of another.[3]

It is humiliating to have to think of persons as members of one family unless the human family as such contains a quality that applies to every person and relates it to all other persons. This quality is the creatureliness of all men. Every human person is conditioned by the fact that it has been created. It has to "accept its own existence as a fact".[4] Every person is therefore a fellow-

[1] C. G. Jung, *On the Relation of Analytical Psychology to the Poetic Art* in *Collected Works*, Vol. 15, London.

[2] It is clear that this is only one aspect of the theatre. It also has a message for the conscious mind. But it will express this most effectively when it calls in aid the "thousand voices" of the archetypes.

[3] Romano Guardini, *Welt und Person*, p. 144.

[4] August Brunner, *Die Grundfragen der Philosophie*, Freiburg, 1949, p. 94.

creature before God. Whereas the encounter between individuals evokes the "Thou-ness" of the person, the experience of human community emphasizes the createdness of every person. It is the existential basis for the true experience of the archetype of the Brother and Sister of the human race.

3.   To feel oneself a brother of man is not to have reached the existential ground of createdness. Therapeutical "communication" shows how greatly the purely emotional differs from the existential. The relationship between the therapist and the patient[1] provides the framework for an intrapsychic space which is filled with the elemental situation of "trouble and help". The relationship is typical and universally valid so that it enables us to study the attitude of any helper to the spiritually afflicted as it were under a magnifying glass.

According to Viktor von Weizsäcker,[2] the "spiritual doctor" is neither a guide nor an interpreter but an "enabler", one who makes things possible. By his very mode of living and behaving he loosens the resistances in the patient and thereby enables the diseased soul to move, to grow and change and to realize itself so that the patient can

[1] "The transfer relationship is at the same time depth psychology's strongest weapon and greatest danger; one is therefore perfectly justified in emphasizing that, therapeutically, the objective and systematic handling of the transfer is the decisive problem." J. H. Schultz, *Seelische Krankenbehandlung*, 1943, p. 150 f.

[2] *Arzt und Kranker*, Leipzig, 1941, p. 58.

become what he was intended to be. In the company of the therapist the patient is able to transfer the actuality to what is implanted and existent in him and achieve a state of health. Psychotherapy calls this process the "therapeutic communication". The coming together of the doctor and the patient creates an atmosphere which in fact proceeds from and is created by the doctor and enwraps the patient. The effect it has on him is usually that he finds himself saying, to his own surprise, things which he has never wanted or has never been able to say owing to various resistances. He feels accepted and at home, moved and sustained by the doctor's vitality. He participates in the doctor's life and this leads to a feeling of confidence, an inclination to discuss sore points, a readiness to show and give himself without a mask. Moreover, this participation in the doctor's world has a constellating force; the problems which oppress the patient come to a head and are prepared for birth as if by the hand of an obstetrician.

The therapeutic communication assumes, on the patient's side, more and more the structure of the transfer in which all kinds of relationships are mingled.[1] The first of these is an emotional sense

[1] Sigmund Freud was the discoverer of the phenomenon of the transfer. He interpreted it as an emotional attachment to the therapist, as a "falling in love", an exaggerated attachment which represents the "vehicle" of the whole treatment. The doctor becomes the centre of the patient's emotions. The treatment should break up these feelings by disintegrating them in a rational discussion. C. G. Jung sees deeper than this. For him the transfer is a projection of archetypes which must be

of attachment to the adviser which flows from the feeling of being understood and accepted. Wrapped in this warm sense of security the psyche ventures out of itself and projects archetypes: Animus and Anima, Father, Mother, Doctor, Priest, Saviour, King. The adviser appears as friend, beloved, fatherly protector, surrounded by mysterious powers. The spiritual doctor is forced into all these roles. He will, however, not fulfil the conscious or unconscious expectations of the patient but will call them objectively by name at the appropriate moment, which, again, causes unpleasantness and gives rise to the opposite projections: the traitor, enemy, deceiver, devil. In this way the adviser makes it impossible for the patient to experience all these spiritual forces and helps him to objectify them. In the violent to and fro of the conversation

objectivized and joined to consciousness. For a time the doctor represents the archetypes. Fritz Künkel sees in the transfer the projection on to the doctor of the demands of early childhood in which the child's demand for love takes the form of a desire to nestle in the bosom of humanity. This infantile attitude has to be transformed in the treatment into a mature capacity for community. The analysis of existence sees in the transfer the healing eruption of a deep stratum which is described as the "We-ness of Being" (Binswanger). The basic form of human existence is not solitude (Heidegger) but an existential relationship between man and man. In the transfer this ontological fact emerges with healing power. See S. Freud, *Introductory Lectures on Psychoanalysis, Collected Works*, Vol. 16, London, 1950; C. G. Jung, *The Practice of Psychotherapy* in *Collected Works*, Vol. 16, London, 1954; F. Künkel, *Das Wir*, 1938; L. Binswanger, *Grundformen und Erkenntnis menschlichen Daseins*, Zurich, 1942.

which takes the form on the one side of a wooing and defying, on the other of an effort to help from a depth into which the patient is to be drawn, the patient undergoes a gradual process of existential deepening. The adviser is not a lover or a saviour after all and he disappoints all the patient's expectations in this regard[1] until he sees through all the projections and asks: "What is the point of my continuing with you?" Only when he has reached this point will he sense his relationship with the adviser as with a fellow-creature, involved in the common destiny of man, a brother or sister of mankind. When this situation has been reached the therapeutic communication suddenly calms down; both partners in the conversation are "on an equal footing on the metaphysical basis of their common humanity."[2]

The eyes of the patient's soul are opened, it sees the doctor as a human being, senses his solidarity with him and is thereby called to enter into this solidarity—the trouble he is in will prevent him from evading the call and he is called to assert his sense of fellowship. He gets a firm footing inside himself, even though it is only on a frontier: the frontier of his createdness. On this spot he is

[1] We are not interested in the present context in all the difficulties and dangers which occur in the treatment of neuroses. We are merely interested in the anthropological, typical happenings that take place in therapeutic communication.

[2] V. E. von Gebsattel, "Krisen in der Psychotherapie" in *Jahrbuch für Psychologie und Psychotherapie*, I (1952), p. 77.

wholly existent, he takes hold of his existence and makes a personal reply to his helper, though in the form of the now genuinely religious question: "What are the prospects of the human race of which we are both members for better or worse?"

Appropriate help[1] is therefore based on two preconditions: (a) knowledge and experience of the archetypes; (b) the existential depth of the helper himself. Person calls to person and both must find each other not in the Thou-ness of love as in the sexual encounter, but in the name of their common creatureliness. The solidarity of their common humanity is the atmosphere in which man can live.

From a psychological point of view the whole process signifies a conflict between consciousness and the unconscious which is the native soil of the archetypes. The process of centring advances in the energetic surge between the projection and the objectivation of the archetypes. Man has come one stage nearer his complete self-realization. How one-sided this psychological view of the process is, is obvious from the fact that no one can say in advance whether a patient will join in the existential movement of the helper. In their secularized terminology psychotherapists call it a matter of "grace". But it is enough if this mystery is related to the mystery of the person which, in spite of its creatureliness, is the creative foundation of its own decisions and actions.

[1] Cf. Hans Wollasch, "Sachgerechtes Helfen" in *Vom Wesen und Walten christlicher Liebe*, Karl Borgmann, Freiburg, 1948, pp. 209-241.

9. SIGNIFICANCE

"GOD cannot thrive in a humanity that is psychic-
ally undernourished."[1] With this statement of
Jung's a note has been struck in psychotherapy
which has made religion presentable again in
psychology. The repression of the religious demands of the soul has often been established as a
cause of illness. Many psychotherapists believe
from their own experience that humanity has lost
its soul and that the psychotherapists must find it
again; only when a patient has made a place for his
religious disposition in the "household of the soul"
will he be cured. Depth psychology has established therefore that the religious predisposition
and its activity forms an essential part of the human
psyche. Psychic culture includes religiousness.

Although religiousness is being increasingly wel-
comed by psychotherapists, opinions about the
"what" and "how" of religion differ very widely.
Some say in relation to this problem: "In really
critical psychotherapeutic work it can never be a
question of striving for general evaluations ... we
must recognize life itself in the greatest possible
abundance, as the ultimate criterion."[2] Jung follows the "religious need" of the individual soul.
After awakening their religious disposition he allows

[1] C. G. Jung, *Woman in Europe* in *Collected Works*,
Vol. 10, London.
[2] J. H. Schultz, *Seelische Krankenbehandlung*, Jena,
1943, p. 248 f.

some to glide back into the bosom of Mother Church, "because they are most suitably and usefully housed there."[1]

He leads those who do not suffer a relapse to a religious formation of an individual nature. He believes the soul is strong enough to create new religious forms and symbols—not collective and universally valid ones, however, but individual ones which take into account the character of the individual. Our age is therefore only at the beginning of a new religious culture. Viktor Frankl writes that the "medical cure of souls" must only lead the patient to the point where he is roused to a sense of responsibility in the sphere of religion. Once that point has been reached the psychotherapist has no further legitimate part to play.[2] The variety of ways in which psychotherapy can "use" the religious disposition makes it necessary to examine its connection with revelation (1-6) and its importance for the realization of faith (7-9).

1. The discovery of the religious disposition in man (a new discovery for secular science) raises the problem of natural religion and its relationship to Christianity. Two things may be said which also apply to the religious findings of psychotherapy:

(a) Modern "natural religion"[3] appears in-

[1] C. G. Jung, *Seelenprobleme der Gegenwart*, Zurich, 1931, p. 430. (The Chapters in this work appear in various volumes of the *Collected Works*.)

[2] V. Frankl, *Ärztliche Seelsorge*, Vienna, 1946, p. 185.

[3] See the explanation of the concept of "natural religion" above, p. 11, note.

creasingly in the most varied forms, even under the guise of the Christian religion itself: in the name of reverent respect for the inscrutable mystery[1] it may be directed against "church routine"; in the name of a human love which calls itself "love for one's fellow man" it may be directed against "rigid dogmas"; it may be opposed to mass religion because it favours a personal relationship to God; and in the name of the "individual religion" it may be opposed to collective religion. In all these forms the problems of faith and doubt are treated "like a branch of psychology". It is maintained that the existence of God depends on the "structure of the inner life".[2] Religion is declared to be a psychological phenomenon, a system of salvation for the psyche. As such it is taken extremely seriously.[3] The inner, and often concealed heart of this attack on Christianity in the name of natural religion is the criticism that Christianity sins against the holy mystery of life and "prevents man from following the religious impulse of his heart and surrendering

[1] Cf. Goethe: *"Das Unerforschliche ruhig zu verehren"*. "Calmly to revere the unfathomable ..."
[2] Olov Hartmann, *Heilige Maskerade*, Frankfurt, 1953. The main character in the novel, the wife of a pastor, records in her diary a visit to a nerve specialist whom she asks "Do you believe that God exists?" He replied that he was not competent to answer such questions, but that it would do him immense good to realize the religion which he carried inside him, that, he said, was something he did understand (p. 111).—See also the present work, p. 91 f.
[3] C. G. Jung, *Psychology and Religion*, Yale University Press, 1936.

to the fullness of the divine".[1] The discovery of the religious disposition in the human psyche is therefore a new stage in the self-defence of the sarx[2] against the irruption of the "light";[3] a very subtle form of defence because it takes place in the name of religion.

Its presuppositions are in the first place a psychologistic conception of man in which the personal stratum of being is not seen; in this view the religious man is under no necessity to be personally responsible for his religious experiences. The second presupposition lies outside psychology for it is directed against "revelation".

(b) From the standpoint of the believer in revelation every expression of the religious disposition is inevitably pre- or post-Christian, that is to say, before the encounter with Christ natural religion is a conversation with the still unknown God who has yet to come,[4] a conversation in which the human partner only has knowledge made up of "primeval revelation",[5] numinous experience, symbolism and thought.[6]

Once the natural religious disposition in man

[1] Romano Guardini, *Offenbarung*, p. 95.

[2] *Sarx* is taken here in the Pauline sense of everything in man that is remote from and hostile to God.

[3] John 1, 4-5.

[4] "The old paganism was a love song to the God who hid himself but whose presence was felt all round. The new paganism is a declaration of war against the one God who has revealed himself." Cf. F. Heinemann, *Neue Wege in der Philosophie*, Leipzig, 1929.

[5] See L. Ziegler, *Überlieferung*, Munich, 1949.

[6] See Romano Guardini, *Offenbarung*, pp. 7-46.

comes up against Christ, however, it not only undergoes a "correction", it not only needs to be developed organically but it has to be "redeemed".[1] Once the process of metanoia, of which we shall be speaking later on,[2] is well advanced, the situation changes and man's natural religious disposition becomes the "nourishing soil", the "ontal basis" for the life of faith and its realization. If depth psychology can assist what is already widely practised in psychotherapy, namely the awakening of the religious disposition which is buried in the psyche, the problem is to give these experiences a home in the Christian sphere.

2. As we have shown above[3] the archetypes of communal life raise the question of the weal or woe of humanity in an acutely existential manner.[4] The numinous is bound up with all the archetypes we have so far dealt with. It has two distinct faces: the *Fascinosum* and the *Tremendum*.[5] The religious

---

[1] Thomas Ohm, *Die Liebe zu Gott, in den nichtchristlichen Religionen.* Krailling, 1950, p. 462 f: "Christianity is not a judgement on all the other religions, since they are not devoid of all value and truth, but it is neither merely a correction or development. It is not simply the fulfilment and completion of other religions. In general and in particular these are all false and bad and have to be overcome. It is impossible for them to develop organically into Christianity. The non-Christians need redemption from their religions."

[2] See below, p. 97 f. [3] See above, p. 75 f.

[4] It must be remembered that the different stages in Individuation pass over into one another and only appear separate for the purposes of a systematic exposition.

[5] Rudolf Otto, *Das Heilige*, Munich, 1947.

problem is fascinating and terrifying, the answers are inspiring and frightening. Both are contained in the myths and religions which are mankind's attempt to solve the problem; both display the archetypes of the religious. As schemata of experience they are symbols of numinous experience and attempts to solve the problem: divine images conceived by primitive peoples, full of gloomy foreboding; Indian and Chinese religious sculpture instinct with horrors of cruelty; bright airy figures of gods on European soil, gracious and jealous at one and the same time; images of the saviour and redeemer and his dark enemy.[1] Light and dark are fused together. The *Tremendum* and *Fascinosum* are mixed with the Good and Evil.

3. This whole heaven of gods and demons has been depopulated wherever a wave of Christianization has passed through a people (at least for a time, i.e. for centuries) and the civilization which has resulted from man's control of nature has led to the final disenchantment of the world.

In depth psychological terms this process has meant a withdrawal of the projection of religious archetypes and their sinking down into the unconscious where they lie buried among the negative results of the Enlightenment unless they are

[1] Cf. Richard Wilhelm, *The Secret of the Golden Flower*, Introduction by C. G. Jung, London, 1931; Evans-Wentz, *The Tibetan Book of the Dead*, Oxford, 1954; Karl Kerényi, *The Gods of the Greeks*, London, 1951; C. G. Jung and Karl Kerényi, *Introduction to a Science of Mythology*, London, 1951.

deliberately worked up into the Christian system. The numinous in the world has remained but the organs for its comprehension have been repressed and this has led to the existential superficiality and the spiritual desolation of modern man. If, however, the land of the psyche is ploughed up by a grave disaster in real life, for example, or artificially by means of an analysis, these organs can be roused to life again, haunting us in dreams, leading to sectarian fanaticism or causing genuine religious anxiety. We propose to discuss two possibilities here: that of a particular trend within psychotherapy and the way of Christianization.

4. The religious disposition that is awakened in analysis demands a place of its own in the economy of the psyche. The task of the objectivation of the religious archetypes is to find a place for it. Its tendency to projection must be recognized. It is argued that God and the devil are now not to be sought without but form part of human nature and it is there that the synthesis must be found between light and dark, good and evil, God and the devil. The "new ethics"[1] of modern man consists in promoting this integration. "Anything that assists the integration of the wholeness centred in the self is 'good', of whatever nature it may be." This even embraces the necessity of "living out the evil implanted in us by destiny, in free responsibility" and "working it up into our own

[1] Erich Neumann, *Tiefenpsychologie und neue Ethik*, Zurich, 1949.

character". Admittedly, in doing so man has to "sacrifice his innocence and straightforwardness" but this is the only way in which he can develop the courage to form his own "individual evaluation" of good and evil and make himself independent of the "collective values" of the old mass religions. By being consciously accepted, evil is "decontaminated" and no longer unconsciously infects the whole environment. What used to be called Satan is now passed off as "the demands of the unconscious in modern dress".[1] The consequences this has for the whole conception of God are drawn without any hesitation. A psyche that is striving to achieve a synthesis in this way contains "a self-revelation of the deity which makes a clean sweep once and for all of the childish ethical conception which tears God's world apart into light and darkness, purity and impurity, health and disease. The creator of light and darkness, of the capacity for good and the capacity for evil, of health and disease stands before modern man in the unity of his numinous ambiguity".[2]

The arguments used by this ethical relativism are restricted to the psychological sphere. They take the psychic sphere as their sole measure. But the personal is condemned to silence if psychic

[1] *loc. cit.* p. 126—This new ethic is intent above all on attacking "conventional morality" in the sexual field. The book is typical of the ethical approach of many psychotherapists. Psychologically it is based on Jung's conceptions but it develops his methodical beginnings into an extreme ethical position.

[2] *loc. cit.*, p. 126.

integration is made the criterion for good and evil. The principle of psychic completeness is thereby isolated and made absurd by being made absolute.

5.   The person turns to the religious archetypes as mere, albeit real images the polluted condition of which is an expression of fallen humanity, and it tries to break through them and their projection to the intended reality. What is left of the numinous, if all the images are recognized to be mere projections and are superseded by it? Man is pushed to the edge of an abyss, he stares out into a "dark night of the soul", the night of Transcendence. Is it the faceless mystery of nothingness or the "desert of the naked Godhead"?[1]

Are good and evil bound up together in this night or is one above and the other below? No one could give a binding answer unless God himself had revealed himself and thereby given the faithful the assurance that the judge of good and evil is not a faceless transcendence but the God who is three persons. His words are the criterion for good and evil, light and dark and a guide for the religious

[1] Mechtild von Magdeburg, *Fliessendes Licht der Gottheit*, quoted by Gertrud von Le Fort in *Die Abberufung der Jungfrau von Barby*, Munich, 1940: "It was as though suddenly all the attributes of God were withdrawn into an inaccessible mystery and she saw a quite alien image of God—no, she could see no image of God at all but only the desert of the naked Godhead" (p. 97). It would be worth investigating how far the mystic stage of purification signifies at the same time the withdrawal of the archetypal images of God, so that nothing is left for the soul with which it can imagine or feel God; it lives in a "dark night".

disposition. But the most important feature of revelation is the *Epiphania* in the second person of the Godhead himself.

6. To begin with, the archetypes of the religious hurl themselves at Christ in projections and take possession of him and all the expectations to which he gives rise. Difficulties and obstacles only arise after closer study. Christ does not behave as a normal son does to his mother (John 2, 4: "Woman, what have I to do with thee?"; Mark 3, 34: "Who is my mother or my brethren?"). His disciple Peter, whom he has chosen to be his deputy, he calls a devil (Mark 8, 33: "Get thee behind me, Satan"). He disappoints the pious followers of the law (Matthew 5 ff: Sermon on the Mount; Mark 2, 23: Plucking the ears of corn on the Sabbath and Matthew 23: the reproving of the Pharisees). He is criticized for keeping company with sinners (Mark 2, 16: "How is it that he eateth and drinketh with publicans and sinners?"). He rejects the political hopes attached to his kingship (John 18, 36: "My kingdom is not of this world"; Luke 23, 37: "If thou be the King of the Jews, save thyself"). He does not use his powers of healing as the people hoped he would (Mark 1, 37: "All men seek for thee"; John 11, 21: "Lord, if thou hadst been here, my brother had not died"). He does not in the least resemble the popular idea of a Son of God (Luke 23, 8: Jesus before Herod; Luke 22, 66: Jesus before the Council; John 19, 5: "Behold the man!" Luke 23, 35: "Let him save himself, if he

be Christ, the chosen of God!"). Jesus stands athwart all archetypes. The reaction against him comes not only from the intellectual, but also from the unconscious, the archetypal, from the natural religious predisposition in man. The whole of Christ's life and words is a "stumbling-block": "But we preach Christ crucified, unto the Jews a stumbling-block, and unto the Greeks foolishness".[1] The more worldliness the catechumen brings in his religious disposition to his encounter with the Gospel the greater will be the natural resistance of the *Sarx*[2], the more he will become opposed to the archetypes and the more projections will be revoked; but at the same time his eyes will be increasingly opened to the person of Jesus, his mystery, his uniqueness. The human person is confronted by the divine person and what else is required except a decision for or against him? Everything which has been learnt in human encounters and personal relationships finds its fruition in the personal decision of faith. Somewhere and sometime the moment should come for everyone in which he is confronted by the person of Christ, face to face, not emotionally or in archetypal conceptions, but existentially: "For or against *Thee*".

The fewer the projections that distort the sight the more the decision will be an authentic and

[1] I Cor. 1, 23.
[2] See M. Schmaus, *Katholische Dogmatik*, Munich, 1941. Vol. II, p. 127: "Nature does not want to be transformed but to traverse its course in eternal return. The super-natural therefore exercises an exciting influence."

free one, that is, the more it will be taken in the personal sphere. How it will turn out is the impenetrable mystery in the meeting between persons which such words as Grace, prayer, *mysterium iniquitatis* are a mere groping attempt to fathom. But one thing is certain. The more the interpersonal sphere is prepared for this decision by a proper catechumenate, the firmer foundation it will provide for the subsequent realization of the faith.

7. The encounter with Christ is a real contact[1] of the human person with a divine person, so that a personal response befits this decision as no other. In the confession of faith and in the commitment to Christ there occurs a "steepening" of all the psychic powers, an awakening at the heart of the person, an increasing knowledge of the Thou-relationship and the creatureliness of the person. It comes to know increasingly who it really is as though it had been called by its own name. In the decision for Christ the person is roused to the significance of its own name. In the commitment to Christ the person is fully actuated, it is wholly existent, it finds itself.[2] The final stage of individua-

[1] See above, p. 16.
[2] According to Kierkegaard the "measure for the self always is that in the face of which it is a self". By stages man attains to his "self-consciousness", the stages varying according to whether man finds himself *vis à vis* animals, or as a master *vis à vis* slaves, or as a man *vis à vis* the State. But the self acquires a new quality when it finds itself *vis à vis* God. Søren Kierkegaard, *The Sickness unto Death*, trans. Lowrie, London, 1941.

tion begins with the personal relationship to the divine person.

8.   The epiphany of God in Christ is from now on the corner-stone on which the process of conversion is based. The subsequent process of "re-thinking" (matanoein)[1] is now related not only to the historical and moral reality of the catchumen, but also to the archetypal in the depths of the soul. Revelation discloses two things. First, that the life of Jesus is the answer to the quest of the natural religious predisposition in man, and, secondly, the extent to which the archetypal foundation is a mixture of right and wrong. In its raw state it is an expression of fallen mankind's bewildered search for religion. The archetypal foundation is "Advent-like" and needs to be based deliberately on the Gospel.[2]

9.   Good and evil are separated into divine holiness and departure from it. Evil assumes the form of the fallen angel, this enemy, with his followers, of which the archetypes of the devil and the demons are real albeit faded images. The archetypes of God are cleansed of all meaningless

---

Cf. also: "Man is man to the extent that he realizes the Thou-relationship to God". Romano Guardini, *Welt und Person*, p. 165.

[1] Mark 1, 15.

[2] Contrary to the belief of Aloys von Orelli this means that the "existential, archetypal natural law of the spirit" can *not* be. Cf. Aloys von Orelli, "Psychotherapie und Seelsorge", in *Zeitenwende*, May, 1951, pp. 676-688.

cruelty, according to the character of God as he appears in the Old and, more especially, the New Testament. All the religious archetypes which found expression in the old myths are lifted out of their uncertainty and defilement and confronted with the uniqueness of the historical event of the life of Jesus so that they may find their criterion therein. The constant appeal to these archetypes through the rites of the Church's year in which the main events of the life of Jesus are re-enacted, has a purifying influence on them. On the other hand, the archetypal foundation proves to be a nourishing soil and fills the mind with vitality and imagination so that faith is enabled to be realized more and more. The "Word of God" sinks like a seed into the Advent-like soil of the unconscious and bears fruit in the life of faith. And in the sphere of depth psychology, too, the truth of the dogmatic axiom: "*Gratia supponit naturam; non destruit, sed perficit*" is demonstrated, only, however, after man has "surrendered his vain glory and imprisonment in self".[1] He finds himself, his nature and his "name" or significance in the personal relationship to the Son of God, but not out of the unconscious.

[1] M. Schmaus, *Katholische Dogmatik*, Vol. II, p. 130.

PART TWO

10. THE CONSCIENCE

IF the question of the psychological position of the conscience is raised in this context, it will enable us to survey the lines we have dealt with so far, that of depth psychology and that of the personal, from a higher point of view.

1. The four stages in individuation bring[1] about a process of centring.[2] The spiritual dispositions and organs subordinate themselves increasingly to the potential centre of the psyche so that it becomes the centre of all decisions and actions. At the same time it contains the synthesis between consciousness and the unconscious. The structure of the individualized psyche may be expressed in the ternary: consciousness—unconscious—self.[3] Anthropologically this signifies the overcoming of the isolation of consciousness which is now referred to a constant struggle with the contents of the unconscious. *Logos* and *Bios*, *Ratio* and the irrational, must be set in relationship to one another

---

[1] I—Thou—We. See above, p. 40.
[2] Cf. the diagram in Goldbrunner, *Individuation*, 1956.
[3] Bearing in mind St Augustine's "psychological doctrine of the Trinity" this ternary suggests a parallel with the Trinity. The unconscious = the hidden Father, who dwells in light inaccessible; consciousness = the Logos; the self = the Holy Ghost who serves the other two.

Biblical Seminary Library
Goshen College - Goshen, Indiana

to complete the "human inventory" which is formed into an organic unity in the self.

The two dimensions of the self mean the same from different points of view. The self stands above all the dispositions of the soul, comprehending them and guiding them.[1]

The self is within, and the discovery of the self is experienced as a deepening of the inner life. Man is able more and more to live and act from his own interior and his own depths. The more this interior core is formed the more he becomes immune to psychological intrusion from without. This is the place where psychology reaches its frontier. The psychic stratum of being is sustained by the personal stratum of being. It is above the psychic or inside it. The self is therefore the psychological setting for the person or, to use a now familiar metaphor, the core of the person. The latter is the responsible vehicle of all psychic material; psychic "completeness" achieves wholeness therein.

This opens up a new aspect of the self. The "impulse to integration which is inherent in everything psychic"[2] is now recognized to be the "deepest essence of the moral disposition". It attains shape in the self and its moral aspect is

[1] Like the mountain traveller who experiences a valley storm while himself on the summit. The soul is mountain and valley alike. Part of it—the self—towers above everything that happens in the valley. The "spiritual storm in the valley" does not thereby lose any of its fury;—man, however, has his "head" above water.

[2] Theodor Müncker, *Die psychologischen Grundlagen der katholischen Sittenlehre,* p. 158.

called the conscience. Conscience is, according to moral psychology, "the function of the whole human personality",[1] as represented by the self.

The first result that follows from this is that the discovery of the self leads to the training of the conscience. The conscious or unconscious process of individuation and the formation of the conscience go hand in hand; both condition one another, influence, promote or disturb one another. There is a mutual relationship between Being and Knowing, between what a man makes of himself, and blindness or openness to the true and the good, to moral values. Religious education should therefore co-ordinate intellectual training in moral laws and standards with the assistance it can give in the process of individuation.

A second result is the extension of the reality and responsibility of the conscience. Individuation prevents a "partial ethic of consciousness" because its four stages are necessary for the functioning of the whole personality. The dissolution of the persona, the proper assimilation of the sexual encounter, the right attitude to communal forms and the conversion of the religious disposition therefore acquire even more significance in the formation of the conscience. Moral responsibility for psychic completeness is required since it is the basis of all ethical behaviour.

2. If, however, the self, the core of the person and conscience are different aspects of one and the

[1] Müncker, *loc. cit.*, p. 30.

same anthropological seat of justice, then the conscience can no longer be regarded as an impersonal "organ" or "voice" or "function".[1]

The person is actuated only by the call of other persons, in encounters, in social and communal life and in its relationship to the person of God. It is only in its loving relationship to God that it becomes wholly itself. In the same measure, its insight into the will of God is awakened, just as a lover feels and knows instinctively not merely what the beloved does not want but what he *does* desire. The experience of the will of God in the conscience rises in the same way above and beyond the commandments, to the creative fulfilment of the plans and desires of the divine person, insofar as the personal relationship is deepened in love. The loving relationship to God gives access to ever new and deeper knowledge of the divine will, positive opportunities for Christian living, and not only, as is usually supposed, knowledge of the list of Commandments. The conscience contains the Thou-relationship to God.

This personal view of the conscience reveals the heights on which the Christian "comes of age". He understands how to administer the goods that have been entrusted to him[2], how to deal with them in his own independent and creative way and he knows how to deal with the talents entrusted to him.[3] "Children of God" have grown up into sons

[1] See Theodor Steinbüchel, *Die philosophische Grundlegung der katholischen Sittenlehre*, Vol. I, p. 249.
[2] Luke 16, 1 f.
[3] Matt. 25, 14-30.

and daughters of God of whom God the Father expects a mature conversation and whom he recognizes as independent partners. When conscience moulds a Christian life in this way, faith is realized.

11. THE LAWS OF PERSONAL LIFE

ALTHOUGH the person is primarily a metaphysical concept, it is inevitable that it should also be used— as has already happened in the present work—to describe the relationships which correspond to the metaphysical person in the realm of psychic experience. The self and the conscience are localized on the psychic plane, but soar beyond the psychic to the place where legality yields to freedom and calculability to creative action. Both spheres must be seen together, they constitute the personal realm; their interplay and relationships are what we mean when we speak of personal life. We propose to collate some of the laws of personal life which result from our previous discussion. In conclusion we shall describe some of the consequences of these laws for religious education.

1. Men differ not only in their predispositions but also in their strength as persons. This is evident from their ethical decisions, the desire for wholeness, for creative freedom, and in their ethical failures, breakdowns and evasion of decisions. The

causes lie in the first place in the unfathomable mystery of the person, and secondly in its dependence on the whole structure of the character which is in its turn a product of natural endowment (constitution)[1] and the individual course of development (healthy, impeded, defective individuation).

2. Religious education must not rest content with the mere discovery that man is a person, with personal predispositions, and the knowledge that all the expressions of his life are sustained by the person. The innermost responsible seat of judgement can be latent, buried, defective or only fragmentarily developed.

It follows that all education ought to aim at the awakening, promotion and development of the embryonic personal life. This can only happen through the educational atmosphere and through individuation.

3. A personal atmosphere will proceed from educators whose own person is fully actuated or who are at any rate moving, consciously or unconsciously, in that direction. The measure of their self-discovery will be at the same time the measure of the personal character of their teaching. Especially for the child the "spiritual atmosphere

[1] Cf. C. G. Jung, *Psychological Types, Collected Works*, Vol. 6, London. A brief guide to the materials of character is provided by J. Goldbrunner, "Über Stufen der Gemeinschaftsfähigkeit", in *Katechetische Blätter*, 77, January, 1953, pp. 32-39.

of the conversation in the home"[1] is of crucial importance.

4. The process of personal development can be analysed psychologically according to the stages of individuation. Its four stages correspond to the typical tasks which life imposes on all of us as well as to the inner process of development which brings about a synthesis between the conscious and unconscious predispositions.

5. The danger of the formation of a persona must be recognized and where necessary its dissolution must be brought about, so that the ego may come up against reality with no deceptive intermediary stratum. The calls which life makes on the person only act on the person directly if they are not broken by the prism of a persona and do not come to the ear of the ego distorted.

6. The encounter acts on the dialogical structure of the human person and awakens its capacity for genuine encounter. Every encounter is a rehearsal for the freely chosen lasting commitment to a partner, whether the partner be another human being or God. Hence the supreme significance of the encounter in religious education. Loving relationships between human beings help to develop the capacity for an authentic encounter with God.

[1] Ernst Michel, *Rettung und Erneuerung des personalen Lebens*, pp. 86 and 72.

Anticipating the fourth stage in individuation, I may add here that God can so reveal his Person to a human being that the second stage in individuation can be omitted. The religious development of some of the saints—e.g. Thérèse of Lisieux—points to this possibility.

7. The existential superficiality of modern society normally prevents the person advancing to its frontier of creatureliness. It is therefore of crucial importance that the Christian should meet a priest or religious teacher whose own existential depth calls to the depths in the other person.[1] This is made more possible by the fact that the relationship between priest and Christian is prepared by such events as birth, marriage, death, sin, illness and recovery.

8. "The spirit bloweth where it listeth." In other words, God is able to rouse a human person to full actuality by calling it by name without a human intermediary and without a mediator. Those who have been entrusted with the preaching of the word of God, however, must promote the achievement of a personal relationship to the God who has been invisible again since the Ascension, both by their own existence as priests[2] and through the word and the liturgy. The more complete the priest's human nature has become through the

[1] See above, p. 80 f.
[2] Cf. Josef Sellmair, *The Priest in the World*, London, 1954.

process of individuation, the more his own person is actuated; the more he has taken hold of his existence, the more fruitful his activity as a mediator will be. His word will bear a powerful witness and generate spiritual life.

9. If the process of individuation reveals the psychological difficulty of self-discovery, from the personal aspect it appears as a goal that is difficult to attain: the fully actuated person in its relationship to God. This implies no less than the mature and cultivated love for the invisible person of God which alone is the sign of a Christian's adult stature. Admittedly, the love of God can be experienced in two forms: as fulfilment, when God grants the consciousness of his presence, and as privation, when God's absence can be felt. In this latter experience the person is actuated no less than in the former.

10. Once the personal attitude has been attained it has to fight against signs of spiritual fatigue. The fact that the psyche grows weary in the personal attitude which accords with its own innermost structure is the most palpable expression of original sin. Again and again it deviates from the "straight line of existence"; it is unable to hold itself like a ball over a fountain. The ascent of the psyche in the Thou-relationship to God is an effort the difficulty of which is experienced by the priest who has to celebrate or preach several times on Sunday.

The grave consequence of this is that so far as the Christian defects from the personal attitude to God he loses his freedom and needs the support of the Law.[1] The education of the conscience will bring about both: training in the standards and laws of morality and the Church and guidance in the formation of a personal attitude.

11. It follows from all this that the personal attitude is very largely attained only by a part of humanity. Many people remain throughout their lives below the threshold of personal decision and exposed to the "humanly-natural modes of encounter of a spiritual-intellectual and spiritual-physical kind". They do not live "personally, but in accordance with a type."[2]

Here is the innermost heart of the misery of original sin. Weakness and guilt meet in the personal sphere. The importance of depth psychology is that it recognizes the innermost weakness of man

---

[1] The polarity of law and freedom can be shown in marriage. Two lovers "know" exactly what one expects of the other, their lives are a mutual gift and joy. But if love ceases they will need the hurdles of the law, which speaks of the indissolubility of marriage and their daily task will be an effort to get used to one another in mutual service. They will then sense the poverty of their relationship compared with what it was when they were in love; they will compare their former freedom with the harshness of the law. The experience of these heights and depths of human relationships is a preparation for the relationship with God and makes those who have been through it thankful for the help of organized church life.

[2] Ernst Michel, *Rettung und Erneuerung des personalen Lebens*, p. 68.

and points to ways of overcoming it. Individuation is a precondition for the realization of faith and the two often act and react on one another.

The problem of religious education is a double one. The priest must guide his partly immature flock sternly and wisely. A major part of his task consists in creating a well-organized church life, without falling into the error of the Great Inquisitor.[1] Within this organization, however, the priest will pass gently over his flock as with a magnet so that wherever there is an embryonic urge to become a person it may be deepened, made resonant and stimulated into self-discovery.

12. In the case of catechumens who are still quite young a personal attitude cannot be presupposed. Children are no doubt capable of isolated personal actions—evoked and developed by the catechete or the teacher, but the core of the person which is still very largely dormant will not be the responsible vehicle of their moral and religious life. Michael Pfliegler speaks in this connection of an ethic of obedience.[2] It will therefore not be possible to base instruction for the first confession on a personal attitude; this would be too much of a strain on the child. Catechizing should aim at punctilious personal actions but it should be remembered that a personal attitude is only in

[1] The Grand Inquisitor in Dostoevsky's *The Brothers Karamazov.*
[2] M. Pfliegler, *Der rechte Augenblick*, Salzburg, 1938, p. 55.

process of development in the child—a process to which, however, the catechete can make a vital contribution.

13.   The "massification" of the highly civilized State goes hand in hand with a loss of personal creativity in social and communal life. Human society no longer acts like a "healing We" (Fritz Künkel), a "process of depersonalization" has set in[1] which is leading to an increasing loss of the personal centre in man which shows itself in its extreme form in hysteria.

The individual is no longer embedded in a healthy society which forms and sustains him. He is more and more dependent on "the Individual way of redemption, the process of individuation".[2] Hence the need for creating a personal atmosphere in the fellowship of the Church and for regarding the cure of individual souls and religious conversation as the great concerns of the pastoral life.

14.   Religious knowledge can only be realized if the problems are raised existentially. Individual instruction and religious conversation must bear in mind and not give challenging answers before the questions themselves have been roused into life.

An answer that is given too early will either not be understood at all, be felt as a burden or lead to the formation of a persona.[3]

[1] Michel, *loc. cit.*, p. 74.
[2] Michel, *loc. cit.*, p. 87.
[3] This is the counterpart to Kierkegaard's view that existential truth cannot be communicated *directly*.

12. PERSONAL EDUCATION

IF the dissolution of an already formed persona is a difficult and long task with which the spiritual adviser is confronted in dealing with adults,[1] it is also important to know where the danger points lie in education, which aid and abet the formation of a persona, so that the necessary preventive measures may be taken.

1. Professional life is most prone of all to stamp a man with a persona. The profession exerts a stranglehold on the psyche. The only way of preventing this is an education which delays professional specialization as long as possible. The aim of education should be not the "expert" but "the person of wide cultural interests".[2]

The broader the scale of human values to which children are introduced the more approaches to the core of the person will be opened. Premature specialization, with the one-sided training of the intellect, hardens the approaches to the person and

---

"Truth is a living condition of concrete being, which takes place when this concrete self comes into action in the cognitive encounter with a thing. The indirect communication of the "Socratic method" has its place here, that is, so guiding the partner in the conversation that he himself finds what it is only possible to find, insofar as the questions have already been constellated by individuation.

[1] See above, p. 44 f.
[2] See Sellmair, *Bildung in der Zeitenwende*, pp. 122-132.

covers them with a persona. Unspecialized cultural education is personal education; prematurely specialized professional education promotes the formation of a persona.

In the field of primary education a decisive change is taking place in the so called "training for wholeness", in the incorporation in the curriculum of all kinds of manual work.

But in Germany the so-called high school where the future university student spends his formative years continues to concentrate on the one-sided development of the intellect just as the apprentice's training is limited to the practical sphere. Neither system embraces the whole human being. As educational factors they both rank behind the family and behind the sphere between the school and the family which is becoming increasingly important: the leisure hours which young people spend in youth groups and clubs. This is a sphere which offers the priest more opportunities for cultural and personal education than are afforded in religious teaching in schools.[1]

Amateur dramatics afford an important opportunity for personal education.[2] The alternating

[1] The educational system in the U.S.A. shows how the school can be better adapted to human development. Education is compulsory up to 18 years. The eight years at the Elementary School and the four years at the High School are devoted less to intellectual training than to all-round growth. Only at the College stage is learning as such given a central place in the curriculum.

[2] "The young person first becomes aware of himself in speaking and acting, he comes to know himself as a person in a special sense and finds it easier perhaps to

portrayal of various roles can have the effect of preventing the imposition of a persona. Drama in school gives the teacher possibilities of influencing the young players in which, however, great educational skill is required. The example of American schools[1] shows how "dramatization" can be used in all subjects, including religion.

2. The levelling influence of "public opinion" is even evident in the classroom. If the class is left to itself the inferior elements will soon determine its tone by their greater robustness and hardly any child will be able to avoid this class spirit. Experience shows that it can suppress the expression of personal life in a class altogether. In the mass people are always below the level of their true selves. When a teacher faces a mass of children informed by the "class spirit" the children's souls are closed to him. He is confronted by a class persona, not by the open faces of his pupils. There

---

find the way to his own personality and to spiritual communion with others through acting in plays". Sellmair, *Bildung in der Zeitenwende*, p. 127.

[1] In American schools dramatization is a well-tried and popular method of education. The teachers are trained in this method in the "Speech and Drama Departments" which are independent faculties in most of the colleges and universities. Many of the lectures and seminars in these departments are compulsory for all students. The three aims of "creative dramatics" are: (1) Co-operation, (2) Self-integration and (3) Self-expression. The American Educational Theatre Association exists to deepen and spread these ideas. It publishes a quarterly journal, *Educational Theatre Journal* (Columbia, Missouri).

is one great possibility of overcoming the class spirit: splitting up the solid block by means of "functional teaching". The constant appeal to the child to co-operate with its own independent work, dividing the class into groups working at separate tables, getting the more gifted children to help the weaker ones will gradually create an atmosphere in which it is easier to speak to the children as persons.[1] And this is the precondition for Christian teaching. In such classes it will be possible to work with groups even in catechizing.

The working notebook has the same effect. Every child must "do" in some way or other everything that is taught in class. By transferring what has been merely heard to some practical activity the intellect is brought into touch with the "stuff" of human nature: the power of the imagination, the will, diligence, the emotions, the creative capacity, etc. Anyone who is required to *do* something is forced to assimilate the subject independently to a far greater extent than when he is merely required to learn it by heart. The percentage of passengers in the class is reduced and it may therefore be claimed that "functional teaching" of which dramatization, group work and the working notebook merely represent three possible applications, serves the realization of religious life. The collective culture which favours the formation of a persona is delayed and the atmosphere needed for personal activity is prepared.

[1] The presupposition is the guidance of the class by a teacher who keeps the reins firmly in his hands.

3. A "religious Persona" has a disastrous effect. It is formed in the family and the boarding school when frequent and habitual religious activity is carried on under sharp control. The school-age child has an ethic of obedience, i.e. "all the partial goals which the teacher sets before the child are not taken up into the child's ethical world but interpreted as a command which the child feels it must endeavour to fulfil."[1] This is the period in which habits are acquired. Religiosity is sustained not by personal actions but by the scaffolding of family custom, of friends or the boarding school. The scaffolding is like a fence round a nursery of young trees. Here the opportunities for individual personal religious activity are nursed. At this stage, therefore, too great a strain must not be imposed on the child. The religious activity which is demanded of it must not be stuck on like a façade.

When excessive demands are made on the child they cover up the child's true religious attitude. Worse still, however, is the reaction this has on the development of personal life; its power of growth is taken away. Whereas it should take root and be firmly established in the unconscious, the growth on the surface is forced, as in a hot-house. The dangers of acquiring a religious persona increases in the period of pre-puberty when self-consciousness is discovered and the ego is formed. Even in strict religious education the pupil must be given the chance of making his own free

[1] See Michael Pfliegler, *Der rechte Augenblick*, p. 55.

decisions, at least by the taking into account of the periods of crisis in which religious activity sinks, and should be allowed to sink, to an indispensable minimum. Otherwise the pupil will be induced, for fear of the consequences of religious inactivity, to continue "joining in", "making a virtue of necessity" and putting on a persona. If this takes place consciously the discord between the authentic and the unauthentic will prove a good soil for the bacillus of scepticism.

If the atmosphere of a family or a boarding school has a very strong religious character, the unwilling pupil may unconsciously identify himself with a persona. Religious education must prevent religious works being performed which are not sustained by a person. This leads, in theological terms, to an exclusive emphasis on "works", and, in psychological terms, to the adoption of a persona.

4. In this connection the daily attendance at Mass acquires a special significance. If the pupils have been prepared according to the principles of modern catechetics the personal relationship to God will stand in the foreground in the Eucharist, not a tract on the value and efficacy of the sacrifice of the Mass. If it requires a special kind of alertness and effort on the part of the adult in order to achieve a full daily realization of a personal relationship to the invisible God, we must seriously ask ourselves whether too great a personal strain is being imposed on children by compulsory attend-

ance at daily Mass. If a child or young person has not the power to sustain a religious activity, such activities will in the long run prove a hindrance to religious growth. If personal life is to enter into religious activities their frequency must be suited to the personal development of the child. The rule should be: "Fewer works and more life in order to create better works."[1]

5.   This will be promoted by the kind of religious instruction which is in accordance with the Gospel call for personal encounter and personal decision. The immanent tendency of Christianity is deeply opposed to collectivism of every kind. Whilst the levelling down of the person is the intended or unintended result of the political and social developments of the twentieth century the Gospel continues to appeal to the person, to its individual decision, its relationship to the Thou, its capacity for encounter. The Gospel has to reach the core of the person through the persona of mass thinking and feeling. The preacher of the Gospel in school and church faces the same situation as the adviser facing the individual whom he wants to help out of his identification with the persona.[2]

Although the religious teacher does not always succeed in reaching the heart of the religious disposition, the catechete does strive to penetrate to the centre of the person at least for a passing

[1] J. Pascher, *Inwendiges Leben in der Werkgefahr.*
[2] See above, pp. 52 ff.

moment.[1] In big classes the tough, dough-like resistance of the collective to personal actions is, however, very noticeable.[2]

The preacher will have an easier time at least to the extent that he has not to cope with disciplinary difficulties. His endeavour will be to speak so that his words appeal to the personal predisposition of his hearers. It is becoming more and more necessary not to address the congregation *en masse* but the individual in the congregation. The style of speaking suitable for wireless sermons seems to be directed to the individual and to be the most suitable form in which to clothe the personal appeal of the Gospel. All the methods of mass suggestion, however, promote persona-like characteristics in the congregation, even if at first sight they seem to ease the preacher's work. Now that the individual Christian lives more and more in an environment of unbelief endurance in the faith requires a pure, deep and personal decision and a religious life nourished from the core of the person. The sermon should provide the struggling Christian with the nourishment he requires and it should therefore be constructed in accordance with the laws of personal life.

[1] Sometimes it only really succeeds for a moment, perhaps in the answering of a question or in the closing prayer. The "situation" plays an incalculable but leading role in class teaching.

[2] Small classes are therefore not only a desideratum for all teaching especially in religion; the extra cost would indirectly yield fruitful results in political life because the susceptibility to the collective could be countered here from the earliest age.

6. The Christian is required by his religion to work very hard on himself. He has to put "off the old man" and put on the "new man",[1] regularly to search his conscience, to prepare for the sacraments, practise asceticism and strive for perfection. The Christian's interest in self-education is therefore very great and there is an extensive literature on the subject to help him.

Human development does not always proceed in a straight line like that of a plant. It is therefore not always possible to say what the next stage will be. There are critical points which may be likened to the chrysalis stage.[2] Neither the patient nor the adviser can say what "butterfly" will emerge from the caterpillar. Such pupations occur above all during the transition from one stage in life to the next.[3] Often a particular ideal only applies to one phase of life; if it continues to be consciously upheld as an ideal in a later phase it may all too easily obstruct the natural development of the person by the imposition of a persona. Theories about self-education ought therefore to lay particular emphasis on the need for trusting the natural development of the person as well as on the

[1] Eph. 4, 22-24.

[2] In the fairy story these times when man no longer knows what's what with himself, are represented as a result of bewitching influences.

[3] According to the Latin tradition, 5 ages each lasting 14 years (i.e. twice 7 years) are assumed as follows:— *puerita*—childhood; *adolescentia*—adolescence; *juventus*—manhood; *virilitas*—mature manhood; *senectus*—old age. Every transition represents a critical period and therefore a special problem for the education of the self.

need for deliberate moulding.[1] In Christian self-education the courage to be oneself should be allied with conscious intervention that is not based on a fixed ideal but grows from a relationship to God based on intimacy with his Revelation in the Bible.

13. THE RELIGIOUS CONVERSATION

THE space between the priest and the Christian is filled with an abundance of inter-personal relationships, to which the religious word is entrusted like a ship which must try and bring its cargo into port in spite of the rolling sea and favourable or unfavourable winds. The factors in the religious conversation which we propose to discuss are (1) the priest, (2) the word, (3) the recipient of the word.

1. In the priest the Christian is confronted with a human being with individual qualities of his own and an official mission. The partners in the conversation brings his mind to bear on the priest in both his capacities. The priest must decide whether, for example, the archetype of the Enemy which the other person may project on him is directed at his office or his person. If it applies to his person he will limit his priestly activity to the necessary minimum until the personal situation is cleared up. His personal idiosyncrasies and his type

[1] See above, p. 41.

will often restrict his influence on opposite types of people. The individual colouring of his words will be felt as an obstacle; as his hearers have not yet penetrated to the heart of the Gospel message his "intonation" may get in their way like a hurdle which they cannot surmount. When this is the case the priest can only serve the Word in all humility. His understanding of the process of projection will not allow him to be personally offended. But if the hostile attitude is directed against his office the way will be open for every possible kind of conflict between light and darkness and the person of the priest will place itself at the disposal of all the tasks of his office without reserve. Pastoral work among girls needs special attention in this connection. Often enough the priest is the involuntary bearer of projections which represent a complex of archetypes[1] in which the archetype of the animus acts in a still undeveloped embryonic state alongside the archetype of the priest. The influence of his individuality becomes mixed up with that of his office, in fact the influence which he may be able to exert by reason of the projection may be astonishingly great. The priest must, however, be able to see the situation clearly and soberly. The youth passes through the years of transition from childhood to maturity. His outlook is still prepersonal but he is on the way to self-discovery and the undifferentiated projections on to the teacher or priest are merely opportunities for self-discovery.

[1] Friend, Father, Brother, Hero, Beloved, Priest, Doctor, Man. See above, p. 82 f.

Young people's religion is also very largely pre-personal and transitional, and therefore as promising as it is fluctuating. If, however, the first experiences of the archetypes are mixed up with religion this represents a great change, albeit one fraught with danger, for the process of self-discovery. The Christian permeation of the person turns the archetypal experiences into bricks from which a view of the world can be built when the period of youth is ended. The mixture of these archetypal experiences with religion can, however, also act as a poison if it is "disappointed" by a wrong attitude on the part of the admired person. Wounded and hostile the archetypes will then turn their whole energy against religion. That is the danger that lurks in a youthful attachment to a priest.

The priest's influence will be disillusioning and poisonous especially if he no longer sees the projection and no longer knows that he has to play a part that has been foisted on him, and comes to enjoy the admiration bestowed on him and finally responds with a "counter-transfer" in which he projects his own ideal on to the child entrusted to his spiritual care and thereby distorts his view of the reality of the child's soul. Even though, as the older person, he may, it is to be hoped, soon catch himself again and attain to greater maturity in the process of overcoming the "temptation" (which is represented by his own anima, not by the girl), the confusion caused in the partner will be incomparably deeper. His anima has evoked her animus out of the complex association of archetypes and this impels the girl to seek a genuine encounter which by reason of his office the priest cannot fulfil. The betrayed animus cuts itself off from the priest and his religion or begins to lead a vagabond life of its own. Because of the possibility of this grave development some priests adopt such a defensive attitude, perhaps after some initial enthusiasm at their success with young people, that no projection appropriate to youth dares to appear, except that of a gloomy, cold or external representative of just such a God.[1]

The problem is really to direct the projection aright. Since his aim is to detach the archetype of the priest from the projected complex, the priest must behave selflessly and with the strictest self-control. The young person experiences this attitude to begin with in all kinds of iridescent colours: the kind father, the radiant and successful man, the understanding friend, the challenging ideal, the mystagogue and compelling preacher in church and among young people. If the priest is sure that he is only doing what his office authorizes him to do and what is necessary for his work as teacher, priest and pastor, then he will be the model on which the life of those entrusted to him will be based. The various archetypes will be differentiated and can gradually be consciously distinguished one from another—the priest may be able to help by

[1] There also exists the teacher who deliberately aims at the awakening of projections in order to taste his power over the souls tied to them.

a word in season—the projections will be taken back[1] and the inner life enriched. The archetype of the priest will be clarified, disciplined by the doctrine of the Christian office of priest, and the young person will be grateful to the priest all his life for the genuine help he has given him. The insight into the "mechanism" of projection and his knowledge of the archetypes which reside in the depths of the human soul will make it easier for the priest to acquire, by experience, the proper priestly attitude. It requires of him a high level of maturity as a man but it also has the retroactive effect of forcing him to develop a personal attitude, for whilst in spirit he strives to emulate the priestly ideal of the Son of God, his humanity is appealed to at all stages of individuation. He is aware of the loftiness of his priestly office and has experienced the difficulties of concretizing it in the human sphere. Human kindness and understanding will follow from this experience.

2.   The vehicle of the religious conversation is the word: revelation and the word that is related to it. Admittedly this word is also subject to changes in emphasis. It is not long ago since the dogmas of the faith were expounded as a sum-total of statements which must be firmly held to be true and which can be proved from the Bible;

[1] If projections of the animus should hold out obstinately either the priest has acted wrongly or there are disturbances in the young person's psyche which may lead to the extreme of hysteria.

the sacraments were extolled as a means of self-sanctification; ethical teaching consisted in commands and prohibitions. The personal relationship to God receded to the sphere of private devotion as a cultivated but purely individualistic relationship.

The new Christocentric thought of recent times has brought a new emphasis on Christ as the centre of the Gospel of salvation, combining a new interest in the Biblical personality of Christ with his reality in the Eucharist. In catechizing on the sacraments the dogmatic teaching that Christ appointed all the sacraments has become predominant (which is no doubt correct but it overlooks the symbolic content in the individual administration of the sacrament).

In revelation, however, only one line runs Christocentrically, the other and more dominant one, is theocentric. The reason why the image of the God-Father has failed to come to life is that the Old Testament has been explained more as the history of the people of Israel rather than the history of God's ways with man. But this is the conception of God which is presupposed in the New Testament. Once the Old Testament is regarded in the light of the Gospel[1] the theocentric line will clearly emerge and greater importance will be attached to the personal relationship to God the Father. This will also make it easier to appreciate the symbolic representation in the sacraments of the relationship between God the Father and God

[1] Cf. Daniel-Rops, *Histoire Sainte: le peuple de la Bible*, Paris, 1946.

the Son. The teaching of the faith is God's call to me, the sacraments are meetings with God; ethics tell me the will of God, his wishes for me.

The preparation of this personal Gospel for use in class teaching, sermons, the confessional and personal conversation is not only the main task of religious education to-day[1] but the constant personal concern of every priest for he can only speak personally if he has already realized his own personal relationship to God.

3. When the priest speaks to men with the personal word he must often first prepare the soil in which he desires to sow the seed of the Word. Only too often he comes up against a complete or partial incapacity for faith and before this is removed there can be no freedom for the personal decision of faith; where one who is already a believer suffers from a like incapacity the practical realization of faith will meet with insuperable obstacles until it is removed.

As a pastor the priest must therefore have a knowledge of the soul which will enable him to help people to become authentic persons; he must encourage and purify their corrupted capacity for encounter; interpret their experiences in social and communal life; help them to see the anonymous and personal numinous powers so that they can

---

[1] The new German catechism is an attempt to meet this need. It is published as *A Catholic Catechism*, Herder, Freiburg, 1957 (distributed in England by Burns & Oates).

hear God call on them by name. Preacher, priest and pastor must all combine in the work of preparing the soil and sowing the Word.

To complete the picture we must not fail to mention the "Enemy" who "sows the tares".[1] The assistance which the priest gives in the process of individuation and the personal preaching of the Word are merely the foreground of the battle in which the contestants are the "Enemy", the *Spiritus Domini* and the human person. The religious conversation will often be of no further avail in the thick of this struggle whereas prayer which tarries in the personal sphere of God himself will be able to provide further help and power.

[1] Matt. 13, 24 f.

DATE DUE

DEC 5 '67			
MAR 4 1969			
NOV 4 1971			
NOV 24 '72			
FEB 9 1976			
MAR 19 1980			
APR 2 1980			
FEB 17 1982			
MAR 15 1984			
APR 24 1993			
APR 19 1996			
FEB 14 2005			
OCT 27 2009			
GAYLORD			PRINTED IN U.S.A.

ics. Franz Mussner . . . . $.95

PL-8   *Chr*   *A B*   Fra $.95

PL-9   *Cur*   *Psy*   Josef Goldbrunner . . . . $.95

BR110 .G613   c.1
Goldbrunner, Josef   100105 000
Cure of mind and cure of soul.

3 9310 00013314 8
GOSHEN COLLEGE-GOOD LIBRARY